EXPLORING

THE WORLD AROUND YOU

A LOOK AT NATURE FROM TROPICS TO TUNDRA

GARY PARKER

EXPLORING
The World Around You

First Printing: January 2003

For information write: Master Books
P.O. Box 726, Green Forest, AR 72638

ISBN: 0-89051-377-5   Library of Congress: 2002105389

Ozone illustrations on page 101 are courtesy of NASA Goddard Space Flight Center Scientific Visualization Studio.

Printed in the United States of America

Please visit our website for other great titles:
www.masterbooks.net

For information regarding author interviews, please contact
the publicity department at (870) 438-5288.

Contents

UNIT ONE:

SPACESHIP EARTH AND THE WEB OF LIFE

Earth was created as a "garden of delight." It was not a corrupt place in the beginning. In this unit, we'll learn what happened to our home to cause bad things to happen, what's in store for our planet, and what we need to be doing in the meantime. We'll explore some of the different "rooms" of our home and find out about the flora and fauna in each.

Building on the Right Foundation; Seeing the 4 Cs

I f you don't live in the country, I hope you have a yard, school grounds, or park nearby, where you can watch flowers blooming, dragonflies chasing each other, or little birds learning how to fly. Maybe there's a pond, or even a ditch, where you can play with the turtles or watch tadpoles sprout legs and grow into frogs.

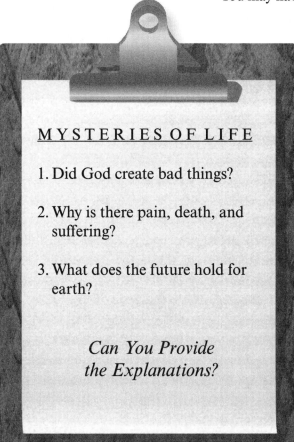

MYSTERIES OF LIFE

1. Did God create bad things?

2. Why is there pain, death, and suffering?

3. What does the future hold for earth?

Can You Provide the Explanations?

You may have thought that the building where you live is your home. But God meant for the whole world to be our home! He created a garden of "delight" (the word *Eden* means "delight") as the home for our first parents, Adam and Eve. God told them and all living things to "multiply and fill" all the wonderfully different "rooms" or environments in our marvelous garden home, the earth.

Ecology is the "study of" (-*logy*) our "home" (*eco-* or *oikos* in Greek). **Ecologists** study the plants and animals on earth and their environments. To get the most enjoyment from our home, we need to know where the different rooms are; how the lights, plumbing, heating, and air conditioning work; where the power comes from; where to find the food; and how to take care of it all. In this book, I plan to take you on a tour of your fabulous home and teach you how it works and how to take care of it — all so you can enjoy it to the fullest and thank God for giving you such a wonderful place to live.

chapters tell us how God created a perfect world. There was no pain, suffering, disease, or death, and no animals or people killing each other. God created all living things working together in perfect peace and harmony, and He told our first parents to "till and keep" (Gen. 2:15) the earth as a "garden of delight."

But in Genesis 3, we learn that our first parents did something that people have been

Wait a minute, you might be thinking. *Sure, flowers and birds and tadpoles are wonderful. But I've been bitten by mosquitoes and scared by poisonous snakes, and I've heard that people have been killed by bears in Yellowstone Park and have had their arms bitten off by alligators in the Florida Everglades. People are always talking about pollution and overpopulation, the ozone hole and cancer, and how global warming is going to make the earth too hot. If God made the world such a wonderful place for us, why do all these terrible things happen?*

The Bible has the answer. The answer is in Genesis, the first book in the Bible. The first two

doing ever since. Like us, they acted selfishly. They disobeyed God. They thought they knew better than God what was right and wrong, what was best for themselves and their world. They rebelled and rejected both God's love and God's Word. In other words, they sinned.

Human sin corrupted (ruined) the world that God had created "very good." Now, mixed in with the beauty and design that tell us about God's wonderful creation, we find the pain, suffering, disease, and death that remind us of human sin. In fact, human rebellion brought so much violence and corruption into our world that God sent a worldwide Flood that de-

Before and after the Fall.

stroyed all the dry land animals and all the people, except those who accepted God's grace and were saved in the ark with Noah. The corruption of human sin and the catastrophe of Noah's flood dramatically changed the world from the way God made it at creation.

Creation followed by **corruption** and **catastrophe** — that's the bad news. The good news is the "fourth C," Jesus **Christ**. God loved us too much to leave us and our world to suffer under sin. He sent His only Son, Jesus Christ, who died for our sin and rose to give us new life, rich and abundant, now and forever (Romans 6:4). And Jesus is coming again to make all things new, a "new heaven and new earth" (2 Pet. 3:13), where "the wolf and the lamb will lie down together" (Isa. 65:25), and we'll live again in perfect peace and joy.

Creation — Corruption/Catastrophe — Christ: a perfect world (1) created by God, (2) ruined by mankind, (3) destroyed by the Flood, and (4) restored by Christ. We'll need to understand this biblical record of the earth's past, present, and future to understand ecology. There are things right with our world that must be preserved and protected, and there are some things wrong that need to be set right. God's stewardship command to our first parents was to **till and keep**, to preserve and protect, to cultivate the promise in each wonder God created. But where things have gone wrong, then, following the example of Christ who healed the lame and blind and restored the withered arm, we need to "heal and restore." Perhaps **heal and restore** is our new ecology command in a "fallen" (sinful) world.

There is another view. In our present fallen world, everyone can see there's pain, suffering, disease, struggle, and death. But people who believe an idea called **evolution** think that struggle and death are normal, that there never was a perfect world created without struggle and death, and there never will be a perfect world in the future that Christ restores. In fact, according to evolution (the "war of nature, famine, and death," as Charles Darwin called it), struggle and death are what made life evolve into all the forms we see today, including us, and it all happened without needing God's help! Struggle and death have been going on for millions of years, says the evolutionist, and struggle and death will continue

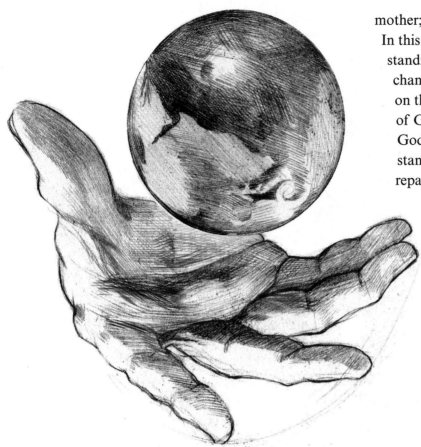

mother; it's the home my Father gave me." In this book, we won't build our understanding of ecology on the fallible, ever-changing words of men (evolution), but on the infallible, never-changing Word of God (Jesus and the Bible). May God grant us the wisdom to understand, and the love to care for and repair, this awesome home He's given us. Let us serve faithfully until Jesus comes to make "all things bright and beautiful" again!

"It's the home my Father gave me."

on earth until the sun burns out and life is no more. According to evolution, the earth is our "mother," and when "Mother Nature" or "Mother Earth" dies, we die.

Evolution says it's millions of years of struggle and death until death wins. The Bible says *life* wins — new life in Jesus Christ!

Praise God, science supports the Bible, and we have reason to live in hope, not despair (1 Pet. 3:15). Even so, a lot of people choose to believe evolution, and it affects the way they view ecology. For an evolutionist, man is just another animal, with no special place in God's plan, and constant struggle to the death, not interdependence and cooperation, is the rule of "nature red in tooth and claw."

But a song my friend Kenny Kirchhavel wrote puts it this way: "The earth is not my

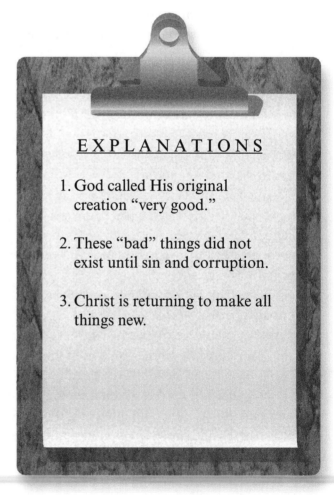

EXPLANATIONS

1. God called His original creation "very good."

2. These "bad" things did not exist until sin and corruption.

3. Christ is returning to make all things new.

1. God created our home, the earth, as a "garden of _____" (the meaning of the word "Eden").

2. What word means "the study of [our] home"?

3. If God created our home in peace and harmony, why do we have mosquitoes, disease, death, and disaster?

4. God's original stewardship ecology command was to "till and _____"; in our fallen (sin-ruined) world, the command, following Christ's example, might be to "heal and _____."

5. Catastrophe, Christ, Corruption, Creation: Put this alphabetized list of the "four Cs" of earth history in correct order from first to last.

6. Associate each of the following with one of the "four Cs" of earth history:
    a. billions of dead thing (fossils) buried in rock layers laid down by water all over the earth
    b. struggle, disease, and death
    c. a perfect world in the past with no pain, suffering, or death
    d. a perfect world in the future, with no pain, suffering, or death

7. What belief says that time, chance, struggle, and death will go on for "millions of years" until finally death wins?

8. What book says that life wins when Christ comes to restore peace and joy forever?

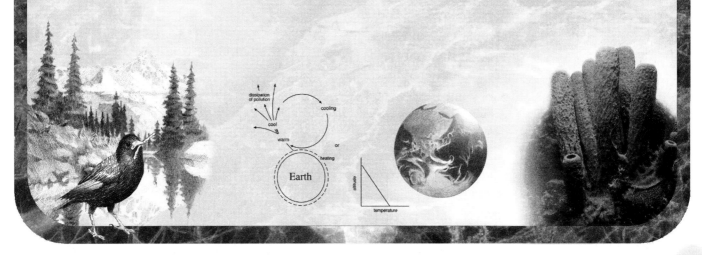

Ecosystems and Biogeography

The basic unit of study in ecology is the ecological system, or **ecosystem**. An ecosystem is a group of plants and animals living together in dependence on each other (interdependence) and their environment.

An ecosystem has two parts: (1) the **biotic** or living part is called the *community*, and (2) the **abiotic**, or physical factors, such as light and temperature, make up the *environment*. In short,

ecosystem = community (biotic, living) + environment (abiotic, non-living)

An ecosystem can be as large as the Great Plains or the arctic tundra, and it can be as small as a pond or mud puddle. A simple aquarium is an artificial ecosystem. The fish and perhaps a snail and some water plants, called algae, make up the aquarium community. Every community also includes some microbes, very important but very tiny organisms (living things) such as bacteria that we need a microscope to see. The

MYSTERIES OF LIFE

1. An ecosystem is like the human body.

2. More marsupials live in Australia than anywhere else.

3. The ostrich, emu, and rhea are similar, but live far apart.

Can You Provide the Explanations?

abiotic or environmental factors include the water temperature, the amount of minerals and oxygen and acid dissolved in the water, and the lighting.

A terrarium is an artificial ecosystem with air and soil for land plants, animals, and microbes. An aquarium or terrarium provides a terrific opportunity to study ecology in action, "close up and personal." If the right ingredients are present, an aquarium can be sealed completely, set in the proper lighting, and it will "take care of itself" for years! The fish and snails feed on the plants and give off carbon dioxide (CO_2) and waste products. Using light energy, the plants absorb CO_2 and nitrogen from the waste products and grow back, releasing oxygen (O_2) needed by animals (and plants, too) in the process. The microbes, unseen and often unsung "heroes," make the animal waste usable by plants, and help to maintain acid and mineral balance in the water.

In a way, our home, the earth, is like a glistening bright blue aquarium-terrarium, circling the sun at just the right distance for the intricate and interdependent mix of plants, animals, microbes, soil, water, and air. All this has an exquisitely balanced harmony designed by God so that life can flourish. Wow!

Spaceship Earth and the Web of Life. Because the earth is hurtling through space with all the "life support systems" required for a long voyage, ecologists sometimes think of our planet as "**Spaceship Earth.**" Rocket scientists planning long trips through space try to copy God's marvelous designs for our space station home.

The Bible compares the people in God's church to the human body (1 Cor. 12:27–28). The body has many parts all working together, each needing the others. An ecosystem is like the body, too. Green plants make food; animals pollinate flowers and transport seeds; microbes recycle so nothing is wasted; etc., etc.! If one part is in trouble, the whole body (ecosystem) is in trouble. All living things are connected to each other like the strands in a spider's web, so Spaceship Earth is also called the **web of life**.

Impressed with evolutionists' beliefs about "millions of years," some say the seven days of God's creation week must have been long periods of time. But, among many other problems, that would put flowering plants on earth long before the insects were designed to pollinate them and would mean constant disruption of the web of life. God created our first parents with mature bodies, all parts in place, and working together. It really seems that God also created the earth's ecosystem mature. God created eco-*systems*, not eco-*chaos*!

Biogeographic Realms. God also created plants and animals to multiply and fill the earth. They spread out first from Eden, then again after Noah's flood from the mountains of Ararat. Although a grassland ecosystem is recognizable as a grassland wherever it is found, the actual species of plants and animals that make up the **flora** and **fauna** (plants and animals) vary from one geographic region to the next. The predominant grazing animals of the grasslands were bison in North America, a wide variety of antelope and other hoofed animals on the African savannas, kangaroos in Australia, and horses in the Asian steppes.

Animals or plants that play similar roles in similar ecosystems in different geographic areas are called **ecological equivalents.** The bison, zebra, kangaroo, and horse, therefore, are ecological equivalents. The African ostrich, the Australian emu, and the South American rhea, all large flightless birds, are also ecological equivalents.

On the basis of broad patterns of plant and animal distribution, six major **biogeographic realms** are recognized: *Palearctic, Nearctic, Neotropical, Ethiopian, Oriental,* and *Australian.* Each realm is isolated from adjacent ones by some major geographic barrier, such as the seas isolating Australia, the Himalaya Mountains separating the Oriental realm from the rest of Asia, and the Sahara Desert separating the Ethiopian realm of most of Africa from Eurasia.

Why are there these geographical differences? Take Australia, for example, home

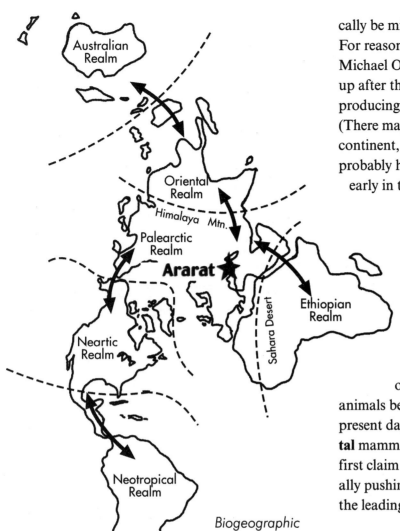

Biogeographic realms

cally be migration from Ararat after the Flood? For reasons given in *The Weather Book* by Michael Oard, vast ice sheets would have built up after the Flood, lowering sea level and producing land bridges among some continents. (There may well have been only one pre-Flood continent, but rapid plate tectonics would probably have begun to break that up into pieces early in the Flood.)

Back to Australia's marsupials. Marsupials seem to be the "kinder, gentler" mammals. For instance, wild wallabies can be petted by tourists on the roadside in Tasmania, and even rabbits (which one would think to be a gentle creature) once threatened to crowd the pouched mammals out of their homeland. So, the idea goes, as animals began to migrate away from Ararat (in present day Turkey), the more aggressive **placental** mammals (those without pouches) would lay first claim to feeding and nesting sites, continually pushing the less combative marsupials to the leading edge of the migration wave. Thus,

of the pouched mammals (**marsupials**), like kangaroos and koalas. Evolutionists once said marsupials evolved there. But fossils show earlier marsupials lived on the other continents, so evolution can't be the answer. Creation isn't the answer either, since God created animals to scatter out over the earth, and they had to scatter out again from the mountains of Ararat after Noah's flood.

Scientists agree that migration is the key, but could it specifi-

marsupials reached Australia first, and God in His providence severed the land bridge they had used so placentals could not follow, and marsupials inherited Australia. They still have to be protected against escaped placental pets and work animals. I've seen the havoc feral cats, dogs, goats, pigs, and camels can wreak among Australia's native plants and animals.

The migration to Australia must have been recent, or other animals would have reached the continent already. The same is true for South America, the Neotropical realm. When European explorers first reached the pampas, there were no large grazing animals despite a most suitable environment. That's hard to explain by millions of years of evolution, but easy to explain as a difficulty for animals having to cross two barriers from Ararat in the relatively short time since Noah's flood.

The "Ararat migration" hypothesis is certainly not proven, but it does seem worthy of scientific investigation.

EXPLANATIONS

1. An ecosystem has many interdependent parts.

2. Marsupials were pushed ahead in the post-Flood migration wave.

3. These birds are called ecological equivalents.

1. What name is given to an interdependent group of plants and animals and their environment?

2. An ecosystem is made up of two parts; the living part called _____ and the non-living part called _____.

3. Give an example of
   a. A large natural ecosystem:
   b. A small, natural ecosystem:
   c. An artificial ecosystem:

4. What can we call a bright blue "aquarium-terrarium" circling the sun at just the right distance for life?

5. Because each part is tied together with all the others, an ecosystem is sometimes called "the _____ of life."

6. According to the Bible (Romans 12), if one part of the body suffers, all suffer. Is that true of ecosystems, too?

7. Thinking ecologically, would it make sense for God to create plants on creation day 3, millions of years before their insect pollinators on creation days 5 and 6? Why or why not?

8. "Flora and fauna" are other names for _____ and _____.

9. Different plants and animals playing similar roles in similar environments in different parts of the world are called _____ _____.

10. Give an example of ecological equivalents in two different biogeographic realms.

11. Different geographic areas including different groups of plants and animals (such as Palearctic, Nearctic, Neotropical, Ethipoian, Oriental, and Australian) are called _____ realms.

12. What continent or biogeographic realm includes most of the pouched mammals called marsupials and few placentals?

13. Did marsupials evolve in Australia? Were marsupials created in Australia? Why do marsupials (like kangaroos and koalas) today live mostly in Australia?

Biomes

Are you ready now to take a tour of your "garden home"? God is the author of variety, and created us in His image to see variety as the spice of life. It's not surprising, then, that God created many different ecosystems for different conditions of *temperature*, *moisture*, and *light* (**climate**). Seven large-scale ecosystems controlled by global climate patterns are called **biomes** (short for "<u>bio</u>logical <u>homes</u>").

Desert, grassland, deciduous forest, tropical rain forest, coniferous forest or taiga, tundra, and chaparral are the seven **terrestrial** (land-based) biomes. The "living skin" of planet Earth, all its land and sea ecosystems taken together, is called the **biosphere**.

<u>Biome distribution patterns.</u> Look for two patterns on a biome map for North America: a south-to-north pattern, and a west-to-east pattern. The west-east pattern represents the effects of increasing moisture for the same general temperature and lighting conditions. As moist air from the Pacific rises over the Rocky Mountains, it drops its moisture, leaving the relatively dry desert regions on the lee side of the mountains. The drier side of a mountain range is called its **rain shadow**. East of the Rocky Mountains' rain shadow, receiving moisture from the Gulf of Mexico and from the north,

MYSTERIES OF LIFE

1. Deserts are not always hot and sandy.

2. Grasslands have no trees.

3. Tropical rain forests are not jungles.

Can You Provide the Explanations?

The drier side of a mountain range is called its rain shadow.

lies the grassland biome called the Great Plains. Still further east, moisture is sufficient to support the life of the deciduous forest, the biome with oaks, maples, and other hardwood trees that lose their leaves in the fall.

A second pattern, from south to north, reflects decreasing average temperature and greater change in seasons in regions which all have a relatively abundant water supply. The tropical rain forest biome in North America covers parts of Central America, parts of Mexico, and the southern tip of Florida. Farther north, in the temperate climatic zone, we meet the deciduous forest biome again, which is part of both patterns. In Canada there is a biome that continues on and encircles the globe through Siberia and northern Europe, the **taiga** or coniferous forest biome, dominated by such evergreens as spruce and fir, which are "ever green" all year. Farthest north is the **tundra**, a vast treeless expanse with lots of water, but this water remains frozen most of the year. The tundra also encircles the North Pole.

South-to-north patterns may be repeated as one moves from the base to the peak of a mountain. Mount Kilamanjaro near the equator in Africa, for example, has tropical rain forest at its base, deciduous forest higher up, followed by a band of coniferous forest, with alpine tundra under its permanently snow-capped peak. As a rule of thumb, each 1,000 feet (300 m) of altitude is equivalent in ecological effects to a northward distance of 600 miles (1000 km).

Grab your imagination and a notepad, and let's take a look at the seven biggest "rooms" (biomes) in the home our Father gave us.

Deserts. **Deserts** do not have to be hot or completely sandy, but they are dry, usually with less than six inches (15 cm) of rain per year. A desert typically has widely spaced water-conserving plants, such as cactus, sagebrush, and juniper. Many desert plants can blossom, pollinate, and shed seeds very rapidly to take advantage of the occasional rain showers. Some animals are also capable of fast development, such as the spadefoot toad, which can grow

The desert biome

are a refuge" (Ps. 104:18).

<u>Grasslands.</u> Enough moisture falls on **grasslands** to support grasses but not trees, although periodic fires are also important in the predominance of grass over trees. It is hard for people who are used to trees to imagine vast open stretches of grasslands, with the nearly ceaseless winds rippling the grass into waves. These areas support great herds of large grazing animals and large predators as well. It's where "the deer and the antelope play" in America (and once, the bison), and where lions chase zebras in Africa. When claimed by man, grasslands become "bread baskets," the most productive farmlands in the

from egg to tadpole to adult within 9 1/2 days, before its temporary rain puddle dries up. It sounds surprising, but because the ground is often hard and doesn't let water soak in easily, deserts are also famous for flash floods.

Animals such as snakes, lizards, kangaroo mice, and mule deer are well suited to desert life, and find their environment no more challenging than forest animals find a forest. (In fact, cacti die if given as much water as our garden plants — they like it dry!) Such a smooth working relationship between life forms and their environment is, of course, no accident; nor is it simply the result of evolution's "survival of the fittest," since an organism must be fit before it can survive! God established the fit of living things with their environment himself. We read, for example, of the wild donkey "to whom I [God] have given the steppe for his home" (Job 39:6), and of the badgers for which "the rocks

The grassland biome

world, easy to till, and with enough moisture for growth, but not enough to wash the minerals from the soil.

Grasslands are called **prairies** or **plains** in North America, **pampas** in South America, **steppes** in Asia, and **savannas** in Africa. The tropical savanna grassland has more trees than other grasslands, and its seasons are marked more by wet and dry periods than by the hot and cold periods of temperate grasslands.

Tropical rain forests. So much moisture falls in **tropical rain forests** that soil fertility is actually reduced because of the washing away of minerals (**leaching**). Nevertheless, species diversity is greatest in this

The deciduous forest biome

biome. For example, in Panama, 141 species of trees have been identified from an area that would boast only 10–15 different species in the eastern United States, and 20,000 insect species have been identified from an area of only six square miles (15 km^2).

Trees are the dominant life forms in the tropical rain forest, and members

Tree stratification, vines, and epiphytes in the tropical rain forest biome.

19

of the violet family, small in other areas, may reach the size of apple trees there. The trees provide food, shelter, and a place in the sun for an incredible variety of **arboreal** (tree dwelling) animals and **epiphytic** plants (those that grow on other plants, such as some orchids), and **lianas** (vines). Mammals, however, are relatively rare.

Because of both the dark shade and the poor soil, ground cover is sparse, and tropical rain forests are *not* jungles. Jungles are usually boundary zones (**ecotones**) between forests and open areas. Neither are tropical rain forests like the temperate rain forests of Tasmania or the coastal Pacific Northwest, where a few tree species dominate.

<u>Deciduous forest.</u> The **deciduous forest** is home to many of the great population centers of the world, such as the eastern United States, western Europe, and eastern China. Its broad-leafed hardwoods such as oak, maple, and walnut,

The tundra biome

have helped to build many civilizations. Although species diversity is less here than in the tropical rain forest, total production in **biomass** (the amount of living material) is the greatest of any biome. Fruits, seeds, and a forest floor covered with decomposing "leaf litter" provide food and shelter for a variety of animals whose number and visibility vary seasonally. The classic characteristics of the four seasons are most obvious in the temperate deciduous forests. "Deciduous" refers to leaf fall, and the colorful autumn display is a spectacular demonstration of God's artistry!

<u>Tundra.</u> A frozen, windswept plain most of the year,

The taiga or coniferous forest biome

the **tundra** comes to life during its long summer days when the ice above the permafrost melts into marshy areas that support tremendous flocks of migratory birds, terrible hordes of mosquitoes, and spectacular displays of blossoming plants. Characteristic residents include the caribou of North America and reindeer of Eurasia, both of which feed in summer on the grassy mats of "reindeer moss," which is really a lichen and not a moss.

Trees, except a few dwarf willows, are absent from the tundra as they are from the grassland and desert biomes. Although water is plentiful, it is available unfrozen for only relatively short periods, and some tundra plants and animals, like desert forms, have accelerated life cycles. The northern robin feeds its young 21 hours a day, and it becomes mature in 8 days rather than the 13 days of southern varieties. During the long arctic summer days, the sun never sets, and local residents take full advantage of the extra daylight.

Taiga or coniferous forest. Conifers are cone-bearing trees (*coni-* means "cone"; *-fer* means "bearing"). They include needle-leaf evergreens such as pine, spruce, and fir ("Christmas trees"). The coniferous forest biome, or **taiga**, is sometimes called the "spruce-moose" biome, because of the prominence of these two life forms. Few living things are equipped to withstand the harsh winters and great snow depths in this biome, and the dominant conifers provide less food and shelter for animals than deciduous trees. But those forms which God has suited for such an environment do well and would actually have difficulty surviving in what we would call milder surroundings! The beautiful and largely unspoiled scenery of the taiga seems to hold a special fascination for those wanting to live close to nature. Trails through the widely spaced trees over a forest floor covered with evergreen needles are usually more pleasant than trails through the bug-infested tangled underbrush of the deciduous forest.

The chaparral and other biomes. Much smaller than the other biomes, the **chaparral**, or Mediterranean biome, is found in Southern California and around the Mediterranean Sea, including the land of Israel, which God called a "land flowing with milk and honey." The nearly endless sunny days and gentle winter rains make

The chaparral

it ideal for people who like outdoor living. Citrus, grapes, and many fruits and vegetables can be grown year around, although irrigation may be required.

The down side is fire. Chaparral plants grow in a semi-arid environment subject to periodic fires, and some plants actually require fire for proper growth and seed germination. The fires that occasionally sweep through regions of California are quite natural. Houses there on wooden stilts with wood shingles are a lot prettier than they are smart. Fire also plays an important role in maintaining the health of certain other forests and prairies, and land managers, once so devoted to fire fighting, are now using "controlled burns" as part of their management programs. We can't be sure whether or not fires were present in the world before sin, but regular mild fires in certain biomes do little harm and a lot of good.

Mountainous regions, as one would suspect, are a mixture of ecosystems, related to differences in altitude and the concurrent changes in climate. Sometimes mountainous regions are simply labeled as **alpine** or **montane** biome. Swamps, marshes, oases, coastal estuar-

ies, and other such **wetlands** are important hatcheries, nesting sites, and migratory stop-overs as ecosystems within each biome.

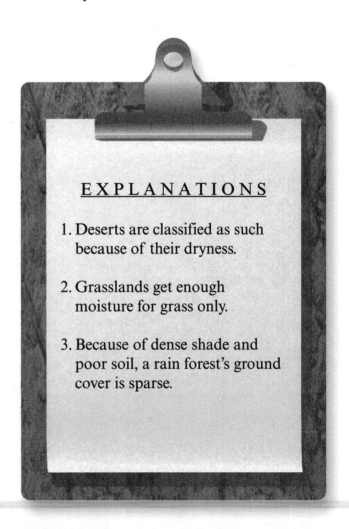

EXPLANATIONS

1. Deserts are classified as such because of their dryness.

2. Grasslands get enough moisture for grass only.

3. Because of dense shade and poor soil, a rain forest's ground cover is sparse.

1. Large-scale ecosystems controlled by global climate patterns are called _____, short for "biological homes."

2. Match the biomes below with each descriptive statement (some terms will be used more than once).

   tropical rain forest   **desert**   **grassland**   **tundra**
   deciduous forest   **chaparral**   **coniferous forest (taiga)**

   a. biome formed in the "rain shadow" of mountains

   b. biome to the north of the deciduous forest, where winters are very cold

   c. treeless expanse with permafrost beneath shallow soil

   d. marshy, with lots of mosquitoes and birds in the summer, when daylight may last over 20 hours a day

   e. less than 6 inches (15 cm) of rain per year, but flash floods are a danger

   f. plants here include cactus, sagebrush, and juniper

   g. the world's "breadbaskets," or most productive farmland

   h. most productive biome; most biomass (amount of life) in a given area

   i. prairies, plains, steppes, savannas, pampas

   j. beautiful autumn leaf color and leaf fall

   k. lots of sunshine, mild temperatures, gentle winter rains

   l. poor soil because heavy rains leach minerals away from roots

   m. fires are normal and produce many benefits

   n. very tall trees with many species, but not much growth on the dark forest floor

   o. "spruce-moose" biome

3. The "layer of life" including all the biomes and aquatic ecosystems is called the _____.

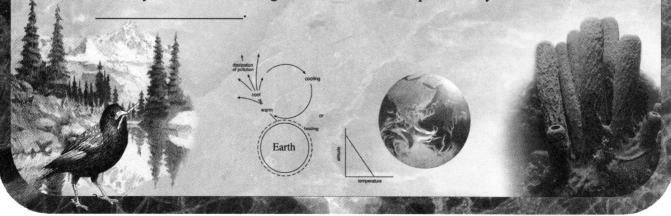

Aquatic Ecosystems

Inland waters. Large lakes have life zones somewhat like those of oceans. Ponds are essentially small lakes with no **aphotic** (lightless) zone. Many large lakes undergo seasonal cycles based largely on the fact that water is most dense ("heaviest") at 39° F (4° C). Water that is *both* warmer *and* cooler will float on top of water that is 39° F (4° C), and water at that temperature will always sink to the bottom.

In the summer, large lakes are layered or stratified, with a warm water layer on top, and a cold layer of about 39° F on the bottom. These two layers are separated by a zone of rapid temperature change called a **thermocline**. Since the warm, lighter water tends to remain above the cold, denser water, virtually no mixing above or below the thermocline occurs. That deprives the upper layer of nutrients and the bottom layer of oxygen.

In the fall, cooling of surface waters causes them to get denser and finally sink to the bottom, causing a circulation of oxygen and upswelling of nutrients called an **overturn.** In the spring, a warming of the icy surface water from freezing to 39° F

MYSTERIES OF LIFE

1. Water in large lakes will turn over every year.

2. The only ecosystem without light still has life.

3. The greatest diversity of life along the seashore is found along rocky coasts.

Can You Provide the Explanations?

Blooms, or high population peaks of algae, often occur at the same time as these spring or fall overturns. It may look like a truck has dumped green paint in the lake, but when viewed through a microscope, "zillions" of one-celled green plants (e.g., *Euglena*) stimulated to growth by the nutrient/oxygen mixing of the overturn can be seen. In the ocean, currents associated with upwellings mark the major fishing areas of the world, such as those off Peru, Portugal, Nova Scotia, and California. Unfortunately, blooms of certain organisms (dinoflagellates) produce "**red tides**," reddish-brown water with a poison that kills fish and spoils beaches.

again causes them to get denser and sink, leading to a second overturn with circulation of oxygen and nutrients.

Many beautiful effects result from God's design for making water most dense at 39° F (4° C), including these two: (1) ice floats, so life survives under frozen lakes in the winter, and (2) both the warming of icy lakes and the cooling of summer lakes to 39° F produce the overturns that stimulate lake growth in spring and fall.

Rivers and streams are a mixture of ecosystems, reflecting differences in current strength, temperature, oxygen availability, type of bottom, and many other such factors. Large, slow-flowing rivers have many of the characteristics of lakes.

Marine ecosystems. Just as the earth's land surface can be divided into several biomes and

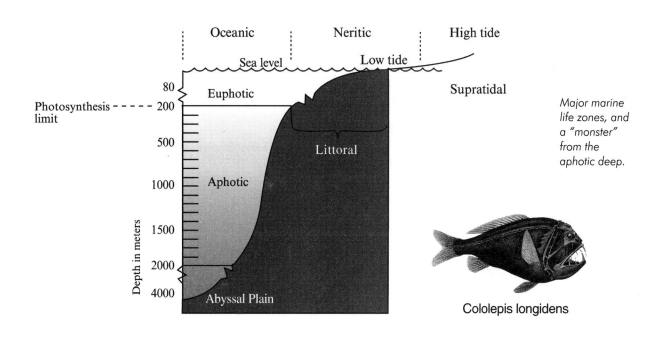

Major marine life zones, and a "monster" from the aphotic deep.

Cololepis longidens

biogeographic realms, so can its seas. We shall comment on some aspects of marine ecosystems below.

Among the more interesting marine areas is the **aphotic zone**, a zone of utter darkness beneath the deepest penetration of light into water. It is the only large ecosystem without green photosynthetic plants, and life there depends on a steady shower of dead and dying organisms, or their waste products, from above. It is a sparsely populated region, but home to some fascinating creatures. The chart on the preceding page includes a drawing of one such "monster" from the aphotic zone, terrifying in appearance until one realizes it can be held in the palm of the hand. For communi-

cation in the aphotic zone, creatures use weird sounds, and some glow, usually because of light-producing bacteria attached to them. Finding a mate can be difficult in such an environment, and in one species the male grows firmly attached to the female as a "parasite," becoming active only to fertilize the egg cells she releases.

Marine animals may be classified as **planktonic** (floating), **nektonic** (swimming), or **benthic** (bottom dwelling). **Phytoplankton**, microscopic floating plants, are abundant in the upper ocean layers, especially over the continental shelves, where mineral nutrients as well as sunlight are available for plant growth. Phytoplankton provide food directly for both microscopic **zooplankton** (animal plankton) and for some huge nektonic forms, including baleen whales. Responsible for 80 percent of the earth's capture of sunlight energy, phytoplankton provide food indirectly for all ocean creatures and, through them, for some life on land. In the middle of the oceans where little mineral nutrient is found even in the lighted

Rocky coastline

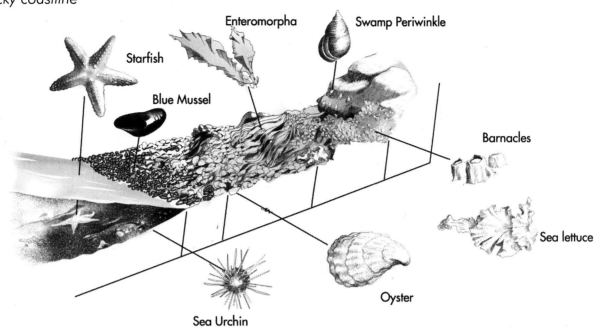

Starfish

Enteromorpha

Swamp Periwinkle

Blue Mussel

Barnacles

Sea lettuce

Sea Urchin

Oyster

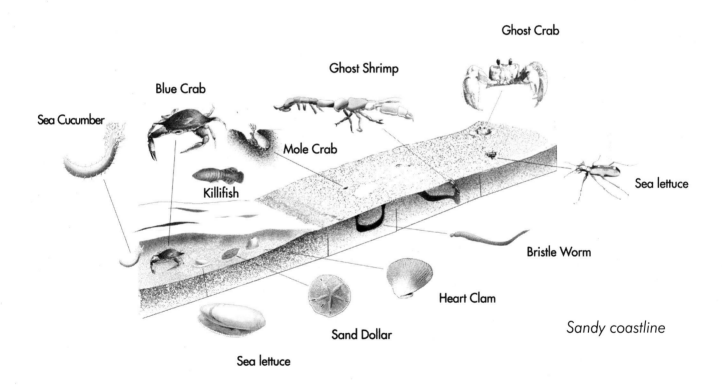

Ghost Crab

Ghost Shrimp

Blue Crab

Sea Cucumber

Mole Crab

Sea lettuce

Killifish

Bristle Worm

Heart Clam

Sandy coastline

Sand Dollar

Sea lettuce

Contrast between intertidal organisms along rocky (top) and sandy (bottom) coastlines.

(**photic**) zone, vast "ocean deserts" exist, nearly devoid of phytoplankton and of the other life forms that depend on them.

Seashores. The kinds of creatures living near the shore and along the coastline are determined primarily by bottom conditions.

Sandy shores do not permit plants to get a foothold, so few permanent residents are found there. Muddy waters often choke filter feeders, again limiting population. The greatest abundance and diversity of life forms are found along rocky shores and the **tide pools** often associated with them, for here both plants and a variety of animals can become firmly attached.

Along a rocky coast, one can usually see stratified life zones reflecting the influence of tides. Intertidal organisms all have some means of attaching firmly, of conserving water while the tide is out, and of resisting wave action. "Rubbery" plants with incredibly sticky holdfasts are found in this region, and clinging animals with wave-resistant shells are common.

Perhaps the most productive of all ecosystems are the **estuaries** where freshwater flows into saltwater. Conditions here seem harsh to us, with the continual changes in water and salt levels. But the constant agitation increases the cycling of nutrients and stimulates terrific growth. Once estuaries were drained as "worthless swamps," and thought to be only suitable for land reclamation projects. Now they are preserved for their beauty, their productivity, and the nesting grounds and hatcheries they provide for many birds and sea creatures.

Reefs. Corals are tiny animals that build limestone cups for themselves, and some can cement huge numbers of cups together to form gigantic undersea "apartment complexes" called **reefs.** Other organisms, like clams and oysters and some sponges and algae, add to the limestone bulk of the reef, forming the foundation of an undersea city that's home to a dazzling variety of fish and many other creatures.

Atolls are circular reefs that often surround a submerged peak.

Fringing reefs are attached to the shore. The biggest reefs are the offshore **barrier reefs** such as the one along the Florida Keys and Australia's Great Barrier Reef. Such magnificent structures would have been destroyed by the worldwide Flood, but calculations based on current rates show there is plenty of time since the Flood for growth of even the 1,000-plus miles (1,600-plus km) of Great Barrier Reef, a spectacular example of God's promise of restoration fulfilled!

Many snorkelers and scuba divers believe the coral reef community is the most stunningly gorgeous ecosystem God created! The reef is characterized by spectacular shades of every color, and body shapes so incredible they stagger the imagination! There are animals called sea lilies that look like plants, except they can get up on their "roots" and walk! All these things show us that God is not only the Great Scientist who put it all together in working order, but He is also the Great Artist who lavishly decorated His awesome creation! We have reason in abundance to praise God for giving us our fabulous "garden home."

EXPLANATIONS

1. Water is heaviest at 39° F, and will sink to the bottom.

2. Aphotic zone creatures feed on waste products showering from above.

3. Sand and mud are not good for most plant life.

1. What is the temperature at the bottom of a deep lake or ocean? Why?
2. Because water is "heaviest" (densest) at 39° F (4° C), mark the following as true or false.
   a. Ice forms on the top of a lake, allowing aquatic life to survive in water below it.
   b. As ice warms from freezing (32° F, 0° C) to 39° F (4° C), the water it forms sinks to the bottom.
   c. As warm water cools to 39° F (4° C), it sinks.
   d. Warming an icy lake in the spring and cooling a warm lake in the fall both produce water that sinks, producing healthy stirring actions called the spring and fall overturns.
   e. If a person treading water was tall enough to span the thermocline in a lake, his/her feet could be cold and arms warm at the same time.
3. Nutrient stirring or inflow plus lots of sunshine and warmth can produce population explosions of algae called _____. One that includes organisms that poison fish and turns the water brownish red is called _____.
4. What's the zone without light at the bottom of a deep lake or ocean called? Without green plants to make food, what do organisms in this zone eat?
5. Match these terms describing ocean life forms: planktonic, nektonic, benthic
   a. floaters, especially small ones
   b. swimmers
   c. bottom dwellers
6. Why are there so many more life forms on a rocky shore than a sandy shore?
7. What do we call large ocean "apartment complexes" formed by corals, clams, and other life forms cementing themselves together?
8. Match the three kinds of reefs with their descriptions: atoll, fringing, barrier
   a. attached to the shoreline
   b. offshore, but parallel to the shoreline
   c. circular, usually around a submerged mountain peak
9. Would reefs have been destroyed in Noah's flood? Is there enough time since the Flood (4,500–5,000 years ago) to grow Australia's Great Barrier Reef (1,000 miles [1,600 km] long and up to 180 feet [50 m] deep)?
10. Do ecosystems show God's fantastic design, fabulous artistry, neither, or both?

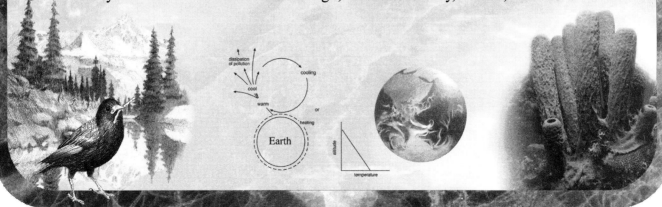

THE ENVIRONMENT: ABIOTIC FACTORS

Now that we've toured the major rooms in our garden home, let's take a closer look at the physical or abiotic factors that are like the "stage props" for acting out the drama of life. The chief abiotic factors influencing ecosystems are light, temperature, water, and minerals. Light and temperature are both involved in the cycle of seasons and in daily cycles. Let's look first at the effect of light on living things.

Light and the Rhythms of Life

<u>S</u>easons. "And God said, Let there be lights in the firmament of the heaven to separate the day from the night; and let them be for signs and for seasons and for days and years" (Genesis 1:14). Artists, poets, scientists, farmers, and most other people are fascinated by the seasons. We understand now that God established seasons by having the earth's axis of rotation tilted with respect to the plane of its orbit around the sun. Because of this, the earth's north pole points most toward the sun in June and most away from it in December, making these summer and winter months in the Northern Hemisphere. It's the opposite in the Southern Hemisphere, where Christmas on December 25 is a summer holiday and Santa is depicted riding a surfboard instead of a sleigh.

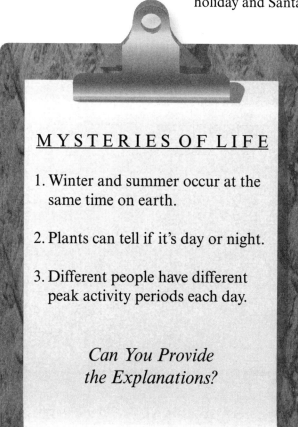

MYSTERIES OF LIFE

1. Winter and summer occur at the same time on earth.

2. Plants can tell if it's day or night.

3. Different people have different peak activity periods each day.

Can You Provide the Explanations?

Although people usually associate seasons with changes in temperature, the most reliable marker of seasons is the relative length of day, or **photoperiod**. Summer begins essentially with the longest day of the year, the summer *solstice*, and winter with the shortest day. Spring and fall start when days and nights are of about equal length (the *equinoxes*). Seasonal effects are much more noticeable toward the poles of the earth than they are near the equator, where, as in Singapore, the days and nights are always

12 hours each. Canadians often enjoy their extended summer evenings when the sky stays light even after 10:00 p.m., but they also have to put up with long winter nights. The illustration below depicts the seasonal variation in photoperiod for selected North American cities.

To measure photoperiod, God gave plants a pigment called **phytochrome** (*phyto* means "plant"; *-chrome* means "color"). The P-660 form is changed to P-730 when the sun comes up. Then it slowly changes back to P-660 after sunset, "ticking off" the length of night.

The more familiar ecological events that depend on seasons are the blossoming and fruiting of flowering plants, and the dropping of fruit, seeds, and leaves in the fall. Many plants regulate the timing of these events in accordance with the photoperiod. Although some plants are **day neutral**, others are either **short-night** (long-day) plants that flower in summer or **long-night** (short-day) plants that flower in either the spring or fall.

Of course, temperatures rise and fall with the seasons, too. But day length is mathematically precise, and it is usually an advantage to a plant to have its seasonal activity related to the photoperiod rather than to temperature. Plants that begin to grow and blossom in response to an early spring warmth may be killed by a late freeze that follows. Nevertheless, temperature does play an important role in regulating plant activity, often in conjunction with the photoperiod.

Sometimes a period of cold treatment called **vernalization** is needed to promote development. Some seeds require a cold thermoperiod before they can germinate and grow. The cecropia moth spins its cocoon in the fall and remains dormant as a pupa over winter. During this time, the cold exposure removes inhibitors to development, and in the spring, the pupa metamorphoses into an adult. If the cecropia moth cocoon were kept in a warm house over winter, it would not develop properly the next spring.

Some animals are suited to meet temperature extremes by either **hibernation** (winter sleep) or **estivation** (summer sleep). Estivating animals include several species of desert rodents. Hibernating mammals include some species of bats, ground squirrels, woodchucks, and jumping mice, but not bears. Real hibernation involves radically reduced pulse and breathing rates and severely lowered body temperatures. But bears are only fitful, sporadically active winter sleepers.

One of the most complicated and fascinating of all processes stimulated by seasonal changes is migratory behavior. Not only do many birds migrate, but so do butterflies, sea turtles, and many other creatures. Some of them travel enormous distances in their migration, such as the Arctic tern which makes an annual round trip from pole to pole, covering about 25,000 miles (40,000 km). Some migrate on very precise schedules, such as the well-known

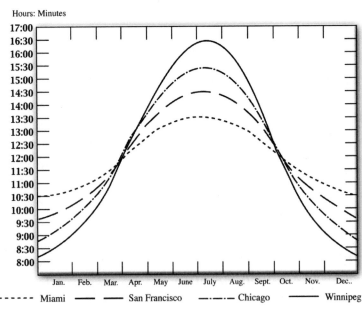

Seasonal variation in photoperiod for selected North American cities.

swallows of San Juan Capistrano. The monarch butterflies are particularly amazing, because one generation migrates from Canada to Mexico, and a different generation migrates back.

The chief regulatory trigger in migration seems to be the photoperiod again, rather than the thermoperiod. In migrating waterfowl, the following sequence occurs. First, the photoperiod is registered by the effect of light on the eyes and/or the pineal gland between the hemispheres of the brain. The day-length information collected is then channeled to a regulatory center in the brain, which stimulates the anterior pituitary gland. The pituitary hormones, in turn, stimulate the sex organs of both male and female birds. The sex hormones released act on the brain to bring about the instinctive migratory behavior.

Understanding computers helps us understand how God could "pre-program" a complex series of events to accomplish a complex goal. Breeding behavior is usually related to this migratory behavior. Normally this system works, in God's providence, so that animals migrate and mate at times of the year best for their survival. Scientists have, however, subjected birds to artificial photoperiods, and induced them to attempt to fly north in January in spite of freezing weather and blowing snows.

One of the many puzzles still associated with migratory behavior is how the migrating animals find their way, especially over great distances. Think of all the navigational equipment it takes to fly an airplane across open ocean from Alaska to Hawaii; God packed the equivalent of all that equipment into a tiny "bird brain." Orientation

with respect to the stars has been suggested, and does seem to work for the migrating sea turtle.

The migration of salmon from the ocean to their breeding grounds hundreds of miles upstream, on the other hand, seems to depend on their sense of smell.

Following landmarks may be involved in some bird migrations, and certain routes such as the Atlantic, Mississippi, Central, and Pacific flyways, are well mapped. Along these routes, extremely large flocks of migrating birds may settle at particular locations at about the same time every year, and these places often draw crowds of fascinated spectators.

Circadian (Daily) Rhythms. "*Circadian*" comes from the Latin for "about a day." It refers to daily fluctuations like the opening and closing of flower petals and the raising and lowering of body temperature and oxygen consumption.

The surprising thing about circadian rhythms is that they persist even when the normal day-night cycle is disrupted. Cockroaches, for example, which have been maintained in either total darkness or total light will

Oh, I can just see them sitting there in their white lab coats, nice and warm in their laboratory.......Just laughing!

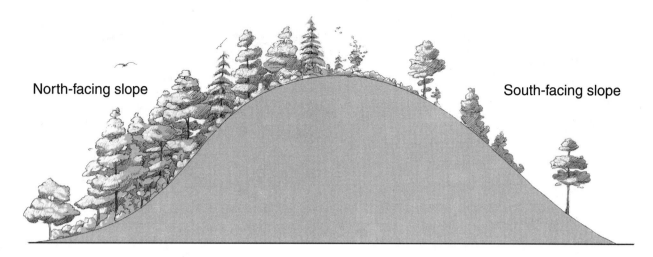

North-facing slope   South-facing slope

still show a maximum activity peak every 24 hours. This daily pattern fades only very slowly, if at all, although it can be reset, at least sometimes, by flashes of light.

People exhibit circadian rhythms. Many have a time of day when they are most active and alert, and other times when they are more lethargic. For "night people," the peak activity period may be reached after the "morning people" have gone to bed. Crossing several time zones on a long jet flight upsets this normal rhythm, contributing to the very real problem called "jet lag."

Some people suffer from SAD (seasonal affective disorder). These people need a lot of sunshine to suppress the melatonin hormone produced by the pineal gland. Since melatonin makes people sleepy, these people have a hard time being alert and active on gray, cloudy days, or during the winter when the days are short and the sun's angle is low. There are now special lights to help these people, although some prefer to travel to sunnier climates during the darker winter months.

Besides seasonal and circadian rhythms, there are also monthly or lunar cycles that seem to be related in some unknown way to phases of the moon. The "grunion runs" (fish spawnings) along the southern California coast is one such example, but there are also many other tales that clearly exaggerate the moon's effect on earth!

<u>Other Effects of Light.</u> Light makes vision possible, provides energy that green plants use to make food, and warms the earth's surface. Since its heating effect varies with the angle at which sunlight strikes the surface, south-facing slopes are much warmer and drier than the shaded north-facing slopes directly across from them. The most important light is Jesus, the Light of the World!

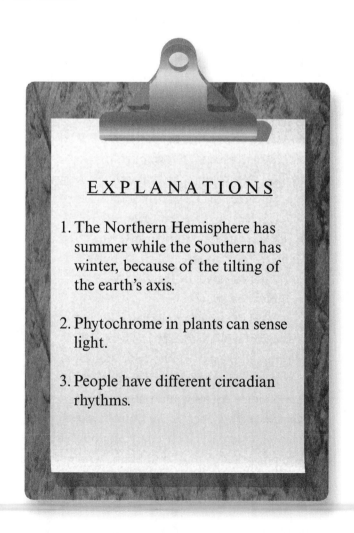

EXPLANATIONS

1. The Northern Hemisphere has summer while the Southern has winter, because of the tilting of the earth's axis.

2. Phytochrome in plants can sense light.

3. People have different circadian rhythms.

1. Are seasons marked more accurately by photoperiod (day length variation) or temperature variation?

2. Which has the longest summer days and longest winter nights: Nome, Alaska, above the Arctic Circle, or Singapore on the equator?

3. What's the function of phytochrome in plants?

4. Name three things in nature whose timings are controlled by photoperiod.

5. Vernalization is a period of _____ treatment that removes inhibitors, allowing, for example, seeds to sprout or insect cocoons to open.

6. "Winter sleep" is called _____. Estivation is _____ _____.

7. Name at least three things that guide migration.

8. How often do *circadian rhythms* repeat? Give an example.

9. Some people are very sluggish during long gray days or the short days of winter when sunshine is scarce, a condition called (by abbreviation) _____.

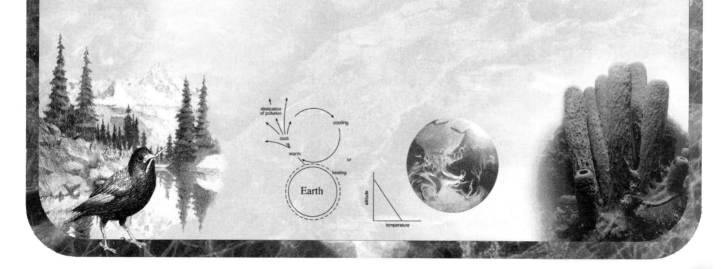

Temperature, Water, and Minerals

Temperature. In addition to its co-function with light as regulator of daily and seasonal cycles, temperature plays several other roles in the ecosystem. Raising or lowering the temperature 10° C (18° F) usually more than doubles or halves, respectively, the rates of chemical reactions (a relationship called the *temperature coefficient* or Q_{10}). Because a little change in temperature can have such powerful effects on how fast or slow living things can function, life is restricted to a narrow temperature range called the **biokinetic zone**, roughly 0°-45° C or 32°-120° F. God designed the earth's atmosphere and distance from the sun just right for life to flourish.

A very important factor in keeping the earth's temperature right for life is the **greenhouse effect**. When it's cold and snowy outside, plants kept in a greenhouse (a building with a glass roof and sides) stay warm and green. The glass lets in the shorter wavelengths of sunlight and plants radiate them back as longer, warmer rays. But the warming wavelengths can't get back through the glass, so the greenhouse "bottles

MYSTERIES OF LIFE

1. Snakes like to lie in the sun on cold days.

2. Virgin Island hotels refund tourists' money if the temperature exceeds 78°F.

3. Fire is a necessary occurrence in some forests.

Can You Provide the Explanations?

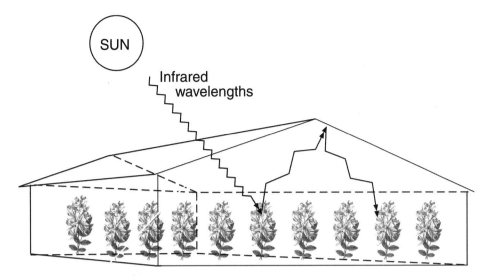

An illustration of the greenhouse effect, by which CO_2 and water vapor especially act as atmospheric blankets, keeping in the solar heat re-radiated from the earth's surface, like glass "bottles up" heat in a greenhouse.

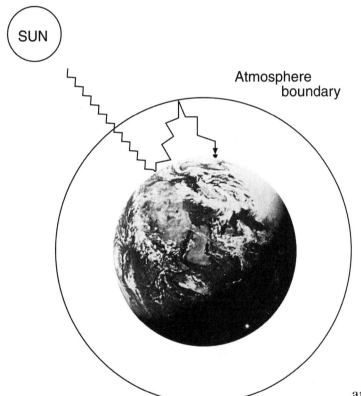

wise even on long winter nights. It gets much colder on clear, dry nights than on cloudy, moist nights because water vapor absorbs the radiated heat. During August in San Diego County, California, temperatures in the desert can swing 50° F (20° C) from a daytime high of 120° F to a pre-dawn low of 70° F (ca. 20°-45° C), but temperatures in the moist air downtown near the coast may change only 15° F (8° C) from 62° F to 77° F (ca. 17°-25° C). Because of humidity changes from coastal fog to desert drought and altitude changes from sea level to nearly 7,000 feet (over 2,000 m), San Diego County has some very extreme changes in ecology over short distances.

CO_2 is also a "greenhouse gas." Some worry that CO_2 will build up from burning fossil fuels, produce **global warming**, melt the ice caps, drown coastal cities, and produce droughts, floods, and famines. We'll talk about that later. We'll also talk about the benefits that greater amounts of CO_2 and the

up" heat and makes a paradise for plants. (If it's too hot and sunny outside, without proper ventilation, a greenhouse can bottle up too much heat and wither green plants.)

The earth is like a greenhouse, and water vapor and CO_2 in the atmosphere act like the glass to bottle up the sun's heat and spread it around, keeping us much warmer than other-

greenhouse effect may have had in the world before Noah's flood.

Homothermal (or homeothermal) (*homo-* means "same"; *-therm* means "heat" or "energy") animals are those that maintain a constant body temperature by internal means, so that environmental temperature changes have very little effect upon them. Birds and mammals are homothermal. They pant or perspire or otherwise lose and evaporate moisture to cool themselves on warm days, and increase blood flow to their surfaces to radiate heat. On cold days, they restrict both water loss and blood flow to the surface to conserve heat, and their bodies' heat production may increase. Fur and feathers help to insulate such animals against temperature fluctuations.

Small animals, which have a lot of surface compared to their size (a high surface-to-volume ratio) tend to have the most trouble conserving heat, and large animals the least. Correspondingly, smaller animals have greater heat production, faster pulse rates, and greater oxygen consumption than larger animals. Heat loss occurs most easily through appendages like legs. For these reasons, ecologists have noticed that varieties of a species with smaller body size are usually found in the warmer parts of a species' range (**Bergmann's rule**); varieties with longer appendages are also found in the warmer parts of a range (**Allen's rule**).

Heterothermal (*hetero-* means "different") or **poikilothermal** animals are those that are unable to regulate their body temperature internally, so they get hotter or colder depending on their environment. Such animals are popularly called "cold-blooded" (in contrast to the "warm-blooded" homotherms), but, of course, they may have quite high body temperatures on warm days.

Lacking precise internal regulation, heterotherms can still influence their temperature behaviorally. Snakes, for example, will sun themselves on cold days to warm up and seek shade on warm days to keep cool. Moths may vibrate their wings in a preflight warm-up period, where the heat derived from muscle contraction warms their bodies sufficiently to allow them to be active. Many heterotherms hibernate in the winter, and when such animals get cold they become very sluggish. A frog kept in a laboratory refrigerator, for example, may be unable to hop until it warms up.

Life forms suited for existence in warm areas are called **thermophiles**; those suited best for medium temperatures are called **mesophiles**; and those that thrive in cold regions are called **psychrophiles** or **cryophiles**. Bacteria and algae living in hot springs are obviously thermophiles. Some of these are **obligate**, which means they cannot even survive at lower temperatures, whereas others are **facultative**, which means they can adjust to other temperatures as well.

Certain creatures such as snow fleas and snow algae survive in snow banks that most people would think incapable of supporting life.

Although there are few other barriers in the ocean, differences in ocean water temperatures restrict the movement of some species. However, ocean temperatures fluctuate

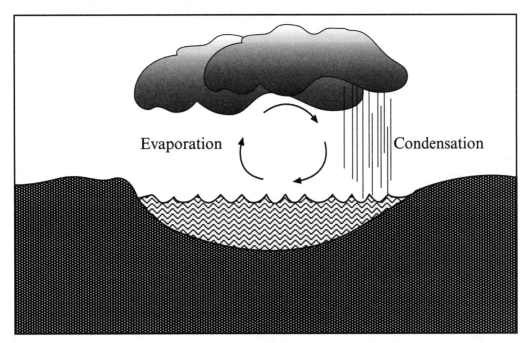

Hydrologic cycle

far less than land temperatures. Shoreline areas and islands also experience lesser extremes in temperature because of the buffering effect of the adjacent waters. Hotels on the Virgin Islands, for example, can safely offer to refund the money of hotel guests if the temperature ever gets either below 68° F or above 78° F (20°-25° C). Ocean currents, by warming or cooling adjacent land surfaces, play a major role in the global distribution of man and other creatures. Southern California is cooled by the Japanese-Aleutian current, for example, and the British Isles, although nearly touching the Arctic Circle, have temperatures not unlike New England's, thanks to the warming effects of the Gulf Stream.

Largely through the manufacture of clothing and housing, man is able to live in many different temperature zones. In addition, some internal adjustment occurs. Among the Eskimos, for example, heat production when they sleep at night actually goes up, rather than down, in contrast to most other people.

<u>Water and Minerals.</u> Water, of course, is a crucial abiotic factor. By adding water, the Israelis and other peoples in arid regions have made "deserts bloom." Water continually comes down from the sky, flowing over and through the land toward the oceans, only to be evaporated into the skies as part of the continual **hydrologic cycle**. Although water is most obvious on the surface or in clouds, water is also present underground. The location of the undulating top of this underground water supply, called the **water table**, helps determine where lakes can form and where plants will grow.

Living things require **minerals** that contain sodium, potassium, phosphorus, nitrogen, sulfur, calcium, magnesium, iron, and even traces of boron, manganese, molybdenum, and others! Where minerals are derived from weathered bedrock, mixed with decaying plant and animal remains (**humus**), and support a thriving microbial community, they form **soil**. Soils can be classified on the basis of mineral and humus content, moisture-holding capacity, texture, and other criteria. Soil is more than just dirt, and helps determine the centers of civilization. Second to climate, soil type plays a

God is the author of variety.

with. God created people, for example, so some prefer the sunny seashore and others the snowy Sierras. God, the author of variety, designed some plants and animals for deserts and others for swamps. They wouldn't "want" to trade places even if they could. Each thrives only when it finds the place designed for it in God's total plan (and there may be a spiritual lesson in that, too!).

major role in determining the climax vegetation characteristic of a given biome. An **edaphic climax** is one determined more by soil factors than by climate.

Water, minerals, and soil type interact in a variety of ways in influencing the distribution of living things. Some soils, especially sandy ones like those in Florida, are quite **permeable** to the flow of water, and the water from drenching Florida thunder showers quickly soak through the ground. Some plants require such easy drainage and greater root aeration, but others cannot obtain sufficient water or minerals from such soils. In soils rich in clay minerals like those in northwest Iowa, water is firmly bound by adsorption to the minerals, and these soils may have a consistency like paste after a rain. They hold onto water and minerals (and boots!) for long periods of time. Many plants would thrive in such a medium, but others would suffocate and die. "One man's meat is another man's poison," as the saying goes.

It's not that one soil type or amount of rainfall is better than another, or easier to live

In areas where rainfall and soil permeability are high, the flow of water removes minerals extensively from the upper layers of soil, a process called **leaching.** Leaching restricts the growth of ground cover in tropical rain forests and on sandy soils. In areas with limited rainfall, calcium salts may form a *hardpan* layer not far beneath the surface, and that can restrict tree growth on prairies.

For many plants, absorption of minerals involves **ion exchange**, or the release of one charged atom (ion) from the plant for every ion taken up from the soil. The ion most often exchanged by plants for soil minerals is H^+, and plants secreting much H^+ tend to make their soils **acid.** In soil with poor water circulation or a lack of acid buffering minerals, the acid build-up can limit growth. But acids also help to dissolve minerals, and some plants grow well in acid soils. Others are suited to grow only in **alkali**, or basic, soils. Farmers may "sweeten" sour (acid) soils by adding lime, and either lime (a base) or vinegar (an acid) may be used to provide the right acid/base balance (pH) for

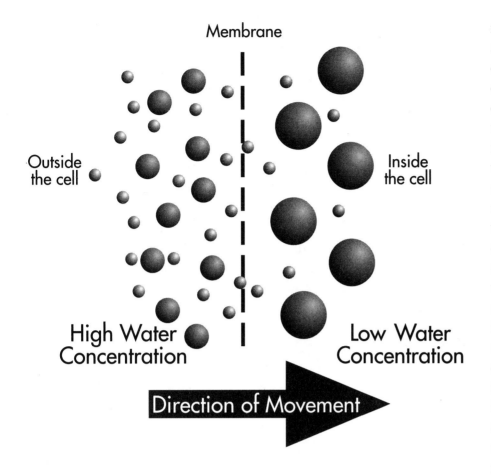

Membrane

Outside the cell

Inside the cell

High Water Concentration

Low Water Concentration

Direction of Movement

move water into cells, and organisms must constantly pump out the excess. Amoebas have contractile vacuoles for this purpose, and freshwater fish excrete a very dilute urine. In the sea, the situation is reversed and the salty water actually tends to dry out organisms osmotically (which is why one can't drink saltwater while waiting for rescue in a lifeboat at sea). Marine creatures excrete a very concentrated urine, and many, including shore birds, secrete salt from their tear glands to help maintain water balance.

Where fresh and saltwater environments meet, we have both **osmoregulators**, organisms capable of adjusting salt balance internally, and

houseplants. Acidity is also important in aquatic ecosystems, and areas with stagnant water or poor drainage, such as bogs, may become quite acidic and unsuitable for many life forms due to the acid released during decay processes — but plants designed by God to "love" acid (acidophiles) move right in!

In aquatic environments, the concentrations of minerals in water, the **salinity** (saltiness), is very important. **Osmosis** is the process that moves water through living cell membranes from areas with more water to less or, said the other way, from less salts to more. In freshwater environments, osmosis tends to

Osmoregulators

Osmosis, natural influx of water into the gills

Diffusion, salt lost from tissue

Large amonts of urine to eliminate excess water from the body

Active re-absorbtion of salt from urine as it is processed in the kidney

Windswept trees

osmoconformers, those capable of surviving as their salt concentrations rise and fall with fluctuations in the environment.

Other Abiotic Factors. Besides light, temperature, water, and minerals, such factors as *gravity*, *wind*, *fire*, and *pressure* affect ecosystems. Gravity helps to orient plant growth on land, but winds may alter this direction somewhat and "stress" the wood on one side of a tree. Wind also helps determine whether an area is populated mostly by winged or wingless insects.

Fire is required to open cones and to release seeds from some conifers and chaparral plants, and fire hastens the recycling of mineral nutrients in prairies, where it also keeps down the growth of competing trees. Pressure is an important factor in the oceans, restricting some forms of life to certain depths, and requiring pressure-adjusting mechanisms in others.

Limiting Factors. All of the abiotic factors described above play important roles in determining the distribution of plants and animals within the biosphere.

Usually one factor is in short supply and restricts growth, so it is appropriately called a **limiting factor.** Even a single mineral can be a limiting factor. Cobalt is missing from Florida soil, for example, limiting cattle weight gain (because it is necessary for microbes in their digestive tracts) until it is added to their feed. Salinity may be a limiting factor in oceans or estuaries, and the extremely high salinity of the

Great Salt Lake and the Dead Sea limit animal populations to *Artemia*, the tiny brine shrimp. A factor in oversupply can also be a limiting factor, such as copper, which becomes poisonous to plants above a certain concentration. In Queenstown, Tasmania, the locals have turned the brightly colored soil under a copper-killed forest into a tourist attraction! Although the concept of limiting factors is easy to grasp, it is often difficult to identify the limiting factor in an actual field situation.

Having looked now at the non-living "half" of an ecosystem, the environment, let's turn our attention to the living "half": the community of living things and their biotic relationships.

EXPLANATIONS

1. Snakes depend on the environment for their body temperature.

2. Ocean currents help keep the temperature constant there.

3. Fire helps some trees reproduce, recycles nutrients, and controls excessive growth.

Questions

Temperature, Water, and Minerals

1. Name two gases in the atmosphere that hold in heat for the earth like glass holds heat in a greenhouse.

2. What might have given the earth a warmer, milder climate pole to pole before Noah's flood?

3. Which animals have body temperatures that go up and down with environmental temperatures — homothermal (warm blooded) or heterothermal (cold blooded)?

4. Write the following terms in order from preference for cold to preference for medium to preference for hot temperatures: thermophile, mesophile, psychrophile or cryophile.

5. An organism that can live only in high temperatures like those of hot springs is a(n) _____ (obligate, facultative) thermophile.

6. An edaphic climax is one determined by _____ (soil, climate).

7. Too much rain can wash minerals away from plant roots, a process called _____. Was this a problem before Noah's flood? Why or why not?

8. Thanks to osmosis, salty water dries out living cells. How do saltwater creatures deal with this problem?

9. The slowest car sets the pace on a one-lane road. What do we call the factor that sets the pace for ecological growth?

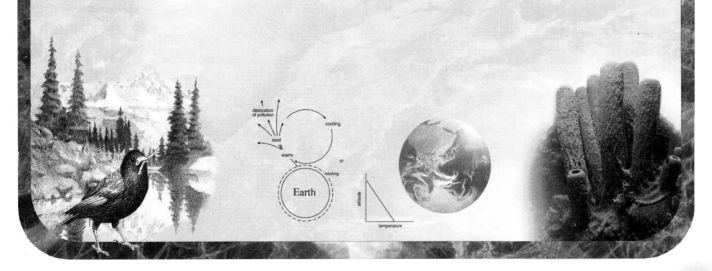

3 UNIT THREE:

THE COMMUNITY: BIOTIC RELATIONSHIPS

Every living organism on earth must interact with other organisms in order to survive. Let's look at those inter-relationships and see how food is created and consumed, how energy flows through food chains, how populations are controlled, and how new communities are created. Along the way, we'll find out why green plants are vital to our survival. We'll see why grain is more important than cattle in many parts of the world, how plants migrate, and why simple organisms like plankton and lichens are important.

FOOD!

Food. Now that's something we can all sink our teeth into! Food supplies the energy for all living things; it's the "gasoline" of life. Second, and just as important, food also supplies the raw materials for building each living body.

The Bible says that people were made from "the dust of the ground" (Gen. 2:7). Sure enough, the simple elements in our bodies are the atoms in dirt, and that's true for the bodies of all plants, animals, and microbes as well. Among the common atoms in living things are carbon, hydrogen, oxygen, nitrogen, phosphorus, and sulfur. Their atomic symbols are easy enough: C, H, O, N, P, and S (Remember the acronym "CHOMPS" but remember to change the *m* to *n*.)

God created green plants both "pleasant to the sight and good for food" (Gen. 2:9). In fact, God engineered these marvelous "green machines" to take simple substances from dirt, water, and air and to build them into food for us and all other living things.

Photosynthesis and Respiration. When God said, "Let there be light" on day 1 of the creation week, He created the energy source green plants used to make food on day 3 even before He created the sun on day 4

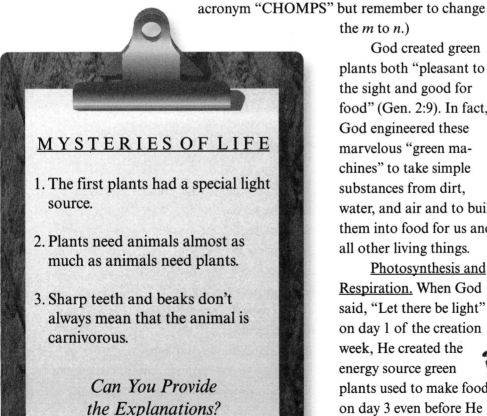

MYSTERIES OF LIFE

1. The first plants had a special light source.

2. Plants need animals almost as much as animals need plants.

3. Sharp teeth and beaks don't always mean that the animal is carnivorous.

Can You Provide the Explanations?

to mark time and to take over the job of showering the earth with light energy.

Green plants are designed to use light energy to put together two common substances, water (H_2O) and carbon dioxide (CO_2), to make the most basic of all foods, the sugar called glucose ($C_6H_{12}O_6$). Because it uses light (*photo-*) to put things together (*-synthesis*), this basic food making process is called **photosynthesis**.

Besides making sugar ($C_6H_{12}O_6$) from water (H_2O) and carbon dioxide (CO_2), photosynthesis also releases into the air an important by-product we all need to breathe: oxygen (O_2) (see diagram at right). The overall chemical equation for photosynthesis can be written as follows:

$$\overset{\text{light energy}}{6H_2O + 6CO_2 \underset{\text{green plants}}{\rightarrow} C_6H_{12}O_6 + 6O_2}$$

In a shorthand way, the equation above tells us that a green plant can use light energy to make one sugar molecule and six oxygen molecules from six molecules each of absorbed water and carbon dioxide.

If you count the numbers of C, H, and O atoms on both sides of the "yield arrow," you will find they are the same. For example, on the left there are six water molecules each with two hydrogen atoms for a total of 12 H atoms. On the

right of the arrow, there is one sugar molecule containing the same total, 12 H atoms ($C_6H_{12}O_6$). Hydrogen atoms were neither created nor destroyed, but just rearranged. That's an expression of one of the most fundamental of all laws of science, the **law of conservation of matter**.

Only God can create something from nothing,

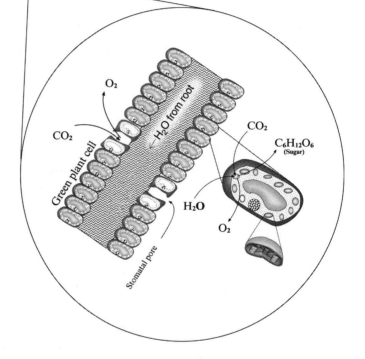

and He tells us that He created all the matter in the universe on the first day of the creation week. *Therefore, conservation is important! Ecosystems must use the same materials (atoms) over and over again, because no new ones are being made!*

So what happens to the sugar and oxygen molecules produced by photosynthesis? Most animals and plants and many microbes use oxygen to "burn" sugar to provide energy for their life processes — growth, movement, digestion, etc. The process of burning food for energy is called **cellular respiration**, and it leaves behind carbon dioxide and water as final products. The overall reaction for cellular respiration may be written thus:

$$6O_2 + C_6H_{12}O_6 \rightarrow 6CO_2 + 6H_2O \text{ (+ energy for life)}$$

Notice anything? Sure enough, the equation for respiration is "equal and opposite" of that for photosynthesis. With arrows pointing in opposite directions, the two equations may be written together as follows:

Photosynthesis (energy absorbed)
$$6H_2O + 6CO_2 \rightarrow C_6H_{12}O_6 + 6O_2$$
$$\leftarrow$$
Respiration (energy released)

That's one reason a balanced aquarium works. That's one reason the earth's ecosystems work. God intricately and ingeniously designed the inner workings of plants, animals, microbes, and people so that the CO_2 and H_2O absorbed to make sugar and O_2 would be exactly replaced by the CO_2 and H_2O released when food is burned for energy. Wow!

Biogeochemical cycles. According to the Bible, God made living things from the "dust of the ground," or elements from the earth, and when living things die (since sin entered the world), their physical bodies "return to dust" (Genesis 2:7 and 3:19). The alternation of photosynthesis and respiration moves substances from the earth through living things and back, so they form a **biogeochemical cycle** (*bio-*, "life"; -*geo-*, "earth"; -*chemical*, "substance"). Almost all people, plants, animals, and microbes are involved in the cycling of C, H, and O atoms. But God established biogeochemical cycles for all the elements, and some depend heavily on a few very important microbes.

Look at the nitrogen (N) cycle diagrammed on the following page. Earth's major storehouse (*reservoir*) of N is the nitrogen gas (N_2) that makes up about 78 percent of the atmosphere.

But green plants can't use the N_2 in the air. A little nitrogen is put into the soil in usable form by lightning, but far more important are the **nitrogen-fixers** — a few blue-green algae (or cyanobacteria) living in the soil, and a bacterium, *Rhizobium*, living in nodules on the roots of legumes such as beans, peas, and alfalfa. Farmers may mix *Rhizobium* spores with bean seeds at planting to make sure there are plenty of these soil-enriching bacteria in the fields.

Ammonia (NH_3) from waste products (that's part of the smell) can be turned into the nitrate form useful to plants ($-NO_3^-$) by two bacteria working one after the other as a "team": *Nitrosomonas* and *Nitrobacter*. If

Alfalfa plant

any pollutant ever killed either of these bacteria, soil fertility would fall dramatically, and food shortages and famines would follow! Never underestimate the importance of even the thinnest strands in God's web of life. To apply 1 Cor. 12:22–25, it seems that God often endows the weaker part, in this case bacteria, with more honor, so that all of the body (ecosystem) is in balanced interdependence.

The nitrogen biogeochemical cycle

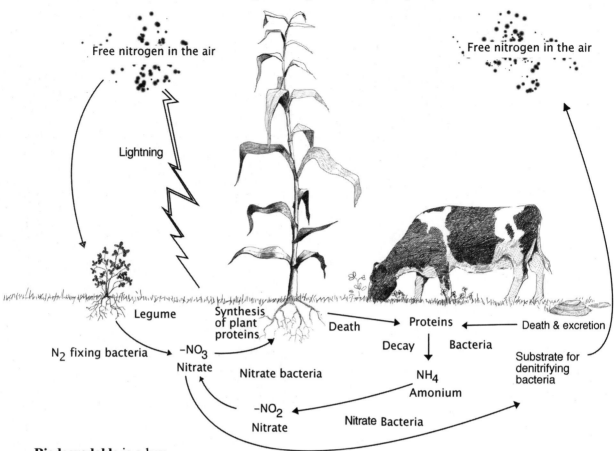

Free nitrogen in the air

Free nitrogen in the air

Lightning

Legume

Synthesis of plant proteins

Death

Proteins

Death & excretion

N_2 fixing bacteria

$-NO_3$
Nitrate

Nitrate bacteria

Decay

Bacteria

Substrate for denitrifying bacteria

NH_4
Amonium

$-NO_2$
Nitrate

Nitrate Bacteria

Biodegradable is a key word today. It means that a substance can be broken down, usually by microbes, and recycled through the earth. **Decomposers** break down dead wood, fallen leaves, and waste products — which really aren't waste products after all, if they are properly recycled. We often say decomposers cause decay, but it's a different kind of decay than the earth's "bondage to decay or corruption" that followed human sin. "Decay" in the sense of the universe growing old and wearing out is bad, and will be set right with Christ's return. "Decay" organisms or decomposers are good; they might be better called **recyclers**, and they have been an important and helpful part of God's plan from the beginning.

Producers and consumers. Because they can use light energy to make food from simple materials absorbed from soil, water, and air, green plants are called **producers.** Living things that depend for their energy and raw materials on the food produced by green plants are called **consumers.** All people, most animals and microbes, and even green plants in the absence of light, are consumers.

Herbivores and carnivores. Consumers include plant eaters or **herbivores** (*herbi-* means "plant"; *-vore* means "eater") and meat eaters or **carnivores** (*carni-*, "meat"; *-vore*, "eater"). An organism that eats anything, such as a teenager, is an **omnivore** (*omni-*, "all"; *-vore*, "eater").

Before sin ruined the perfect and peaceful world God had created, there were no carnivores and all consumers were just herbivores, feeding directly on plants (Genesis 1:28–30). The Bible makes it plain that death, including animals killing each other, was not part of our world until after Adam's sin (Rom. 6:23, etc.).

But, one may be thinking, *what about all those animals with sharp teeth and claws?*

The grizzly bear with its sharp teeth and huge claws is included in a group of animals classified as carnivores. Yet it may surprise you to learn that 80 to 90 percent of what a grizzly eats every year is just fruits and other plant parts. The big claws? They can snatch salmon out of a river (or a camper out of his sleeping bag!), but they are also used to rake through the ground digging up meadow lily bulbs, one of the bear's favorite foods. The flying fox, a big bat so-named because of its vicious-looking teeth, uses its "carnivorous" teeth only for ripping and slashing into bananas, mangoes, papayas, and other such fruits. (Could the teeth of *T. rex*, which are a similar shape but larger, have been designed for tearing into watermelons and cantaloupes?) A hawk is often described as having a powerful hooked beak and sharp claws for ripping up flesh, yet parrots use their "mean-looking" claws and *very* powerful hooked beaks to hold seeds and pry them open.

Many other examples show us quite clearly that sharp teeth and big claws can be used for feeding on *either* meat *or* plants. When man's sin brought struggle and death into God's world, some animals began to use their sharp teeth and big claws to kill other animals, but many continued to use them just to eat plants. In the new creation restored by Christ, once again "the wolf and the lamb will lie down together . . . and the lion shall eat straw like the ox" (Isaiah 65:25).

In some sense, carnivores are degenerated herbivores. The carnivore's digestive system is far less complex, and it can't get all its nutrients from the usual plant sources.

Even human beings may have lost some of the structures and nutritional abilities God gave us at creation, and that (plus dramatic changes in the environment) may be one reason God said to Noah, "As I gave you the green plants to eat, so now you may eat meat" (Gen. 9:3). Although absent from the original creation, carnivores have important roles to play in God's plan for our present, sin-ruined world (as we'll see later).

One might think, *Don't plants die when they're eaten? Wasn't that death before Adam's sin?* Not really. Plants don't die because they're not really "alive" in the biblical sense; that is, they don't have the "life force" (*nephesh* in Hebrew) that God gave to animals and people. If a boy bit his pet dog, it would yelp, feel pain, and try to get away. Nothing like that happens

when one bites into an apple. There was no death of animals or people before Adam's sin, but plants don't have that biblical *nephesh* life.

In fact, God created plants "good for food" and even made them so that they thrive on being eaten! Pruning bushes and cutting grass makes the plants grow hardier than ever. Many plants depend on animals to distribute their seeds, and "entice" them to eat their luscious fruit so the seeds pass through and get deposited elsewhere, complete with a bit of "fertilizer."

As a dramatic example, consider the dodo bird and calvaria tree. About 300 years after the huge dodo bird became extinct on the Indian Ocean island of Mauritius, it was noticed that no calvaria trees had sprouted for 300 years. The only thing that could scratch through a calvaria seed so that it could sprout was the gizzard of the dodo bird!

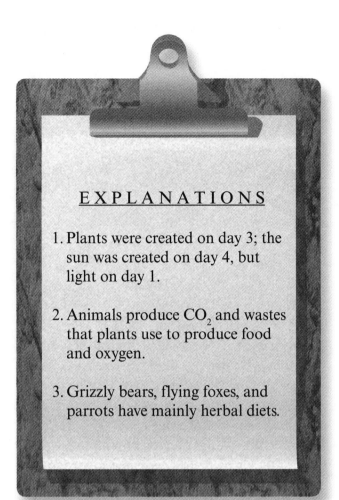

EXPLANATIONS

1. Plants were created on day 3; the sun was created on day 4, but light on day 1.

2. Animals produce CO_2 and wastes that plants use to produce food and oxygen.

3. Grizzly bears, flying foxes, and parrots have mainly herbal diets.

? Questions
Food!

1. According to Genesis 2:9, God created plants both "_____ to the sight and good for _____."

2. *Photo-* means "light" and *–synthesis* means "to put together," so the process God designed for green plants to combine carbon dioxide (CO_2) and water (H_2O) to form sugar ($C_6H_{12}O_6$) and oxygen (O_2) is called _____.

3. Chemical equations show raw materials to the left of an arrow and products to the right. The equation for photosynthesis shows that green plants use sunlight energy to combine six molecules of _____ plus six molecules of _____ to produce (the "yield arrow") one molecule of _____ and six molecules of _____.

4. The equation for photosynthesis shows that the raw materials on the left include six carbon atoms. How many carbon atoms are there in the one molecule of sugar ($C_6H_{12}O_6$) in the products on the right? Were any carbon atoms created or destroyed? Compare the number of hydrogen atoms on the left ($6H_2O$) with the number on the right ($C_6H_{12}O_6$). Were hydrogen atoms created, destroyed, or just rearranged?

5. Chemical reactions don't create or destroy atoms; they only rearrange the way they are put together to form molecules. Scientists summarize that concept in the "law of _____ of _____."

6. When the cells of people and other living things burn sugar with oxygen (carefully!) to produce energy, the process is called *cellular* _____.

7. In cellular respiration, using six oxygen (O_6) molecules to burn one sugar ($C_6H_{12}O_6$) molecule produces six molecules of _____ and six molecules of _____. Is cellular respiration the "equal and opposite" of photosynthesis (the same molecules changing in different directions)? Since God designed photosynthesis and respiration for perfect balance, the number of carbon, hydrogen, and oxygen atoms on the earth _____ (increases, decreases, stays the same).

8. According to the Bible, God made living things from the "dust of the ground," or elements of the earth, and when living things die (since sin entered the world), their physical bodies "return to dust." Science calls this cycling through life (*bio-*) and the earth (*geo-*) of "the dust of the ground" (-*chemicals*) _____ cycles.

9. In the nitrogen biogeochemical cycle, what is the earth's major storehouse (reservoir) for nitrogen atoms? What do we call bacteria and algae that can take nitrogen out of the air and put it in the soil? What would happen to the earth if something harmed the team of two bacteria that change nitrogen in waste products into a form plants can use?

10. If living things (*bio-*) can break down (-*degrade*) a substance and recycle it, the substance is described as _____.

11. The earth would be buried under waste products and dead wood if it weren't for bacteria, fungi, and other _____ that can break them down (decompose them).

12. True or false: The "bondage to decay or corruption" (Rom. 8:21) that followed human sin is bad and tears things down. The recycling by "decay" organisms is good and helps build things up.

13. In food chains, the green plants that *produce* food are called _____; the organisms that eat or *consume* food are called _____.

14. Consumers that eat plants are called _____-ivores; consumers that eat meat are called _____-ivores; consumers that eat anything are called _____-ivores.

15. According to the Bible, were there any carnivores in God's perfect world before sin? Can animals with sharp-pointed teeth just be plant eaters? Give two examples. If big claws are not used to kill other animals and rip them apart, what else can they be used for? Give two examples. When Christ comes to restore our sin-ruined world to the way He wants it, will there be predators killing other animals?

16. Does a plant die when it's eaten? Is that death before Adam's sin? Why or why not?

Energy Flow

Food chains and webs. A list of "who eats whom" in order from producer to consumer is called a **food chain**. Here's a simple example:

Grass → Cricket → Frog → Snake → Hawk

Grass is the only producer above; the other four are consumers. The cricket is the only herbivore; the other three consumers are carnivores. The hawk can be called a **top carnivore** because it's not ordinarily eaten by anything else while it's alive.

In the real world, of course, things usually eat, and are eaten by, several other things, forming a **food web**, perhaps the most basic part of the larger web of life. In the food web on the next page, try to identify the herbivores and carnivores, and those omnivores that can be either.

Biological magnification. Unfortunately, food chains and webs tend to increase or magnify the effect of some pollutants for top carni-

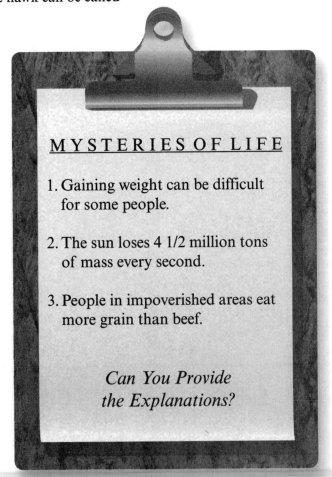

MYSTERIES OF LIFE

1. Gaining weight can be difficult for some people.

2. The sun loses 4 1/2 million tons of mass every second.

3. People in impoverished areas eat more grain than beef.

*Can You Provide
the Explanations?*

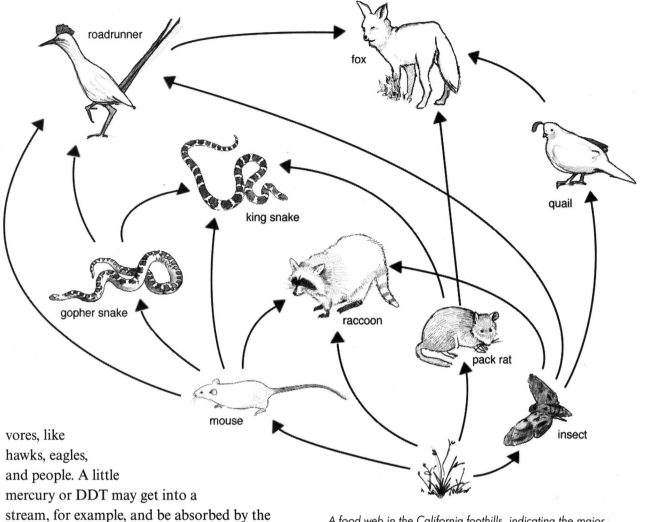

A food web in the California foothills, indicating the major role predators play in our fallen world.

vores, like hawks, eagles, and people. A little mercury or DDT may get into a stream, for example, and be absorbed by the plants that, in turn, have a little mercury or DDT in their cells. But once in a cell, some pollutants, like mercury or DDT, can't get back out. The fish that eats the plant gets a little poison from each plant it eats, but since the poison can't get back out, the poison builds up in the fish to higher levels than it was in its plant foods. The fish which eats the fish which ate the plant accumulates even more pollutant from each fish it eats. Finally, an eagle or person catches and eats the fish that ate the other fish, which ate all those "poisoned" plants. By this kind of "**biological magnification**," an eagle or person fishing in a wilderness area with little pollutant in the water can get seriously poisoned. The excess DDT has caused eagles to lay thin-shelled eggs, and excess mercury — even sometimes from fish in Florida's Everglades or a

Canadian wilderness river — has made people extremely sick or worse. Understanding ecology can be a life and death matter!

Food Pyramids and Energy Flow. Although people constantly on a diet will find this difficult to believe, it's scientifically (if not personally!) very hard to gain weight. A farmer usually has to supply a calf with 10 lbs. (or kg.) of food for each 1 lb. (or kg.) of weight gain. Up to 90 percent of the food energy available to "build beef" is wasted in the processes of chewing, digestion, moving in search of food, etc. Pigs are more efficient, building about 20 percent of food into flesh (80 percent waste), and turkeys better still at 30 percent or three lbs (or kg.) of weight gain for 10 lbs. (or kg.) of food. People vary, but each person has to eat at least 3,500 calories *more* than he or she burns

Top Carnivores

much shorter "plank" for herbivores. Successively shorter planks for each carnivore level give the structure its pyramid shape, with the top carnivore often like a little antenna on top.

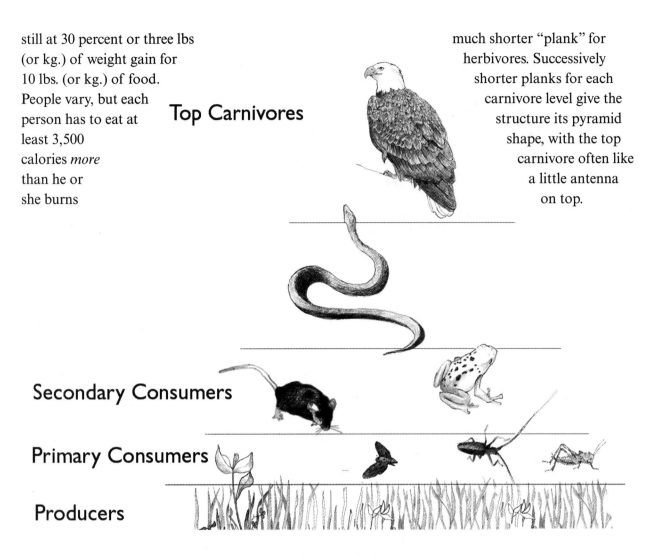

Secondary Consumers

Primary Consumers

Producers

A generalized terrestrial food pyramid

up before there can be a 1 lb. (454 g) weight gain. ("Junk food" makes that easier for people than for most animals, except pets.)

The "energy waste" involved in changing food into flesh means that the usual environment has lots of producers (green plants), many herbivores (crickets, grasshoppers, caterpillars, squirrels, etc.) feeding on the plants, and very few top carnivores. A pair of hawks need several acres to catch enough food for themselves and their young. These energy relationships can be diagrammed as a **food pyramid**.

The base of a food pyramid is a broad "plank" representing the number, mass ("weight"), or energy of all the producers in a given area. The next **trophic** (feeding) **level** is a

Because of tremendous size variation among herbivores (e.g., cricket v. elephant) and carnivores (e.g., preying mantis v. tiger), pyramids of mass (weight) and energy are much more useful scientifically than pyramids of number. Still, as a rough example, a grassland that supported 1,000 crickets would support perhaps 100 frogs, 10 snakes, and 1 hawk.

The figures above illustrate the **10 percent rule**. As a very rough average, only about 10 percent of the food from one level is turned into flesh at the next, while 90 percent is wasted in the search for food, chewing, digestion, heat production, etc.

The Second Law of Thermodynamics. The Bible says that the world is in a "bondage

PYRAMIDS OF MASS

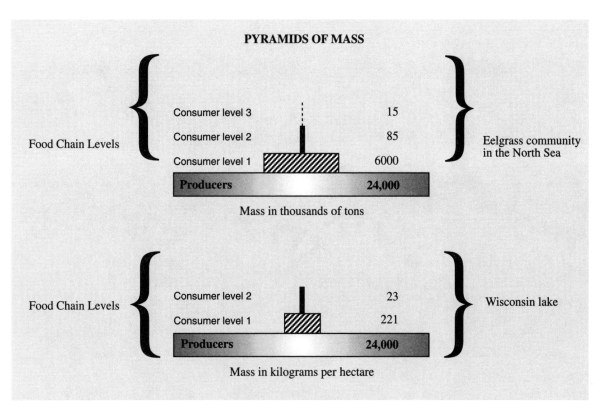

Food Chain Levels

Consumer level 3   15
Consumer level 2   85
Consumer level 1   6000
Producers   24,000

Eelgrass community
in the North Sea

Mass in thousands of tons

Food Chain Levels

Consumer level 2   23
Consumer level 1   221
Producers   24,000

Wisconsin lake

Mass in kilograms per hectare

PYRAMIDS OF ENERGY

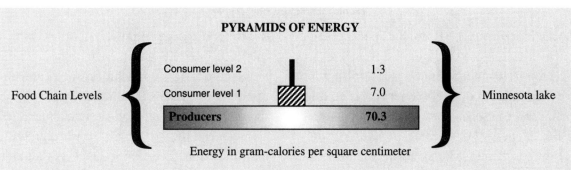

Food Chain Levels

Consumer level 2   1.3
Consumer level 1   7.0
Producers   70.3

Minnesota lake

Energy in gram-calories per square centimeter

PYRAMIDS OF NUMBERS OF INDIVIDUALS

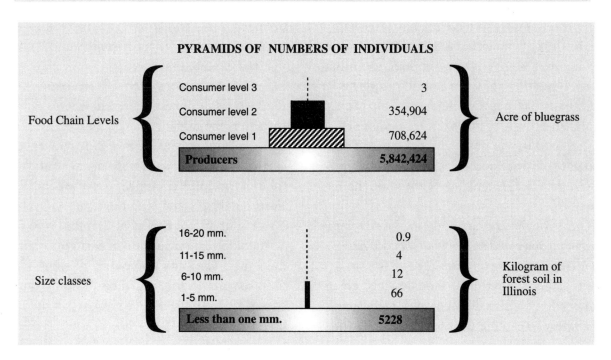

Food Chain Levels

Consumer level 3   3
Consumer level 2   354,904
Consumer level 1   708,624
Producers   5,842,424

Acre of bluegrass

Size classes

16-20 mm.   0.9
11-15 mm.   4
6-10 mm.   12
1-5 mm.   66
Less than one mm.   5228

Kilogram of
forest soil in
Illinois

An example of the second law in action.

to decay [corruption]" (Rom. 8:21) and that the heavens are "growing old and wearing out" (Heb. 1:10–11). Science agrees, calling this continual loss of useful energy, order, and information the **second law of thermodynamics** (*thermo-*, "energy" or "heat"; *-dynamics*, "motion" or "flow"). Illustrations of the second law can be seen all around every day: one's room is easy to mess up, hard to clean up; birthday candles burn shorter, not longer; driving makes the gas tank emptier, not fuller; water flows downhill, not uphill; people and stars grow older, not younger; etc., etc.! In short, all orderly systems left to themselves in nature tend to run down and wear out. The 10 percent rule and food pyramid relationship also reflect the second law of thermodynamics.

But, one might be wondering, *if everything is running down and wearing out, how do living things keep growing on earth?* The answer is green plants and sunshine. God designed green plant cells with incredibly complex molecular machinery to capture the sun's energy and turn it into food energy to power all other living things. If one puts gas in a car, then — thanks to its man-designed machinery — it can run uphill. If one puts sunshine in a green plant cell, then — thanks to its God-designed machinery — it can run life — "uphill," toward growth and multiplication. The second law says that all the growth and increase in the order desired can be obtained *if and only if* there are two things available: an *outside* energy source, and a *system* that can capture that energy.

For earth's ecosystems, green plants are the systems designed to capture energy, and the sun is the outside energy source. But how does the sun replace the energy it showers on earth? *It doesn't.* The sun is burning out; 4 1/2 million tons of it disappear every second! Fortunately, the sun is so huge that — even burning up useful energy at that fantastic rate — it could still power life on earth for many millennia. The sun's doom may be slow, but it's also sure. Eventually, the sun would burn out (Heb. 1:10–11) and life on earth would be no more.

Praise God, that's not the end of the story. There will be another Son, the Son of God. Before our sun burns out, the Son will come to make a new heavens and earth. There the Son will be all the light (Rev. 21:23). The Son of God never burns out, but shines on and on forevermore! "Even so, come Lord Jesus" (Rev. 22:20).

Until that blessed time, however, the second law rules our fallen world, and that has very important practical consequences. Take poverty, for example. Poor people in many parts of the world live on a very re-stricted vegetarian diet that often leaves their bodies deficient in protein and certain key vitamins. The result is often stunted growth, both mental and physical. "Why don't they use some of their plant food to raise beef or pork or turkey?" one might ask. Remember the second law and the food pyramid? For some families, the choice is very simple. If they had a 100 lb. (or kg.) sack of grain, they could feed it to a calf and hope to gain 10 lbs. (or kg.) of meat. Or they could eat the 100 lbs. (or kg.) of grain themselves. Some families just can't afford to waste 90 percent of food they could be eating to enjoy a little meat. It even takes a cow a *lot* of feed to produce a *little* milk.

To test your grasp of food pyramids and the second law, try this problem. Assume you have just crashed on a deserted island. You have plenty of fresh water, one ton of wheat, and a cow. Which of these choices would provide you with the most total food energy:

A. Kill the cow and eat it, then eat the wheat.
B. Eat the wheat while feeding the cow until the wheat runs out, then kill the cow.
C. Feed the wheat to the cow, drink the milk until the cow quits giving or the wheat runs out; then kill the cow.

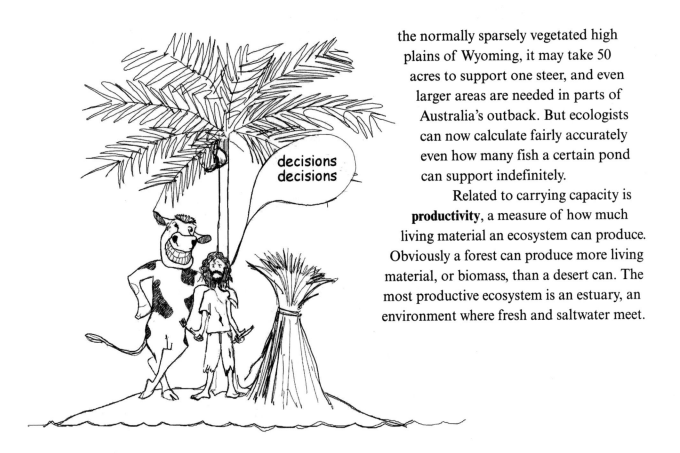

decisions
decisions

the normally sparsely vegetated high plains of Wyoming, it may take 50 acres to support one steer, and even larger areas are needed in parts of Australia's outback. But ecologists can now calculate fairly accurately even how many fish a certain pond can support indefinitely.

Related to carrying capacity is **productivity**, a measure of how much living material an ecosystem can produce. Obviously a forest can produce more living material, or biomass, than a desert can. The most productive ecosystem is an estuary, an environment where fresh and saltwater meet.

Neglecting quality of food, variety of diet, etc., the thermodynamically correct choice is A. If you feed the wheat to the cow, it wastes nine pounds (or kg.) out of every ten either making meat or making milk, making choices B and C incorrect. And if you wait to kill the cow without feeding it, it loses weight from burning energy for heat, breathing, etc. The best choice was not given: planting the wheat to harvest the sun's energy, so you can keep the cow, drink the milk, and have a nearly endless supply of food for both you and the cow!

<u>Carrying capacity.</u> On the more practical side, food pyramids and the second law also help farmers and ranchers figure out how much life a given area can support, i.e., its **carrying capacity**. If the carrying capacity of a grassland for cattle is exceeded, for example, the cattle will eat up the grass faster than it can replace itself, and the whole range will be damaged. Overgrazing and overcropping (along with below-normal rainfall) produced the awful "dust bowls" in the 1930s. In

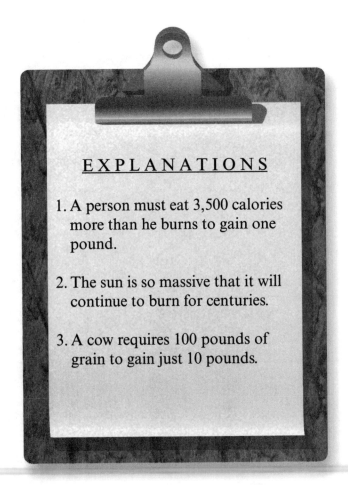

EXPLANATIONS

1. A person must eat 3,500 calories more than he burns to gain one pound.

2. The sun is so massive that it will continue to burn for centuries.

3. A cow requires 100 pounds of grain to gain just 10 pounds.

1. List these in proper order to form a food chain: carnivore, top carnivore, herbivore, producer.

2. Environmental poisons that build up in the body, like DDT and mercury, are found in greatest amounts in _____ (producers, carnivores). This process is called "biological _____" because the effect of poisons increase, or magnify, up the food chain.

3. If a food chain were diagrammed as a food pyramid to show different amounts (numbers, mass, or energy) in an area, which of the four levels from question one would form the broad base of the pyramid? Which would form the tiny peak at the top?

4. The Bible says the world is in a "bondage to decay or corruption" (Romans 8: 21) and the heavens are growing old and wearing out (Heb. 1: 1–11). Science agrees, calling the continual loss of useful energy, order, and information the _____ _____ of thermodynamics.

5. Using the 10 percent rule and the second law of thermodynamics, how many tons of grass would it take to raise 100 tons of cattle? Using this figure, ranchers can calculate how much area it would take to raise those cattle, a measure of that area's _____ capacity.

6. If a poor family decided to feed grain to young cattle instead of themselves, how much weight gain in beef could they expect from every 100 lbs. (or kg) of feed? Do you see why poor families are likely to eat more bread than beef?

7. According to the second law of thermodynamics, things *left to themselves* run down and wear out, *but* living things can grow and multiply if they have *both* an outside energy source *and* a system to capture that energy. What's the outside energy source for life on earth? What living things were created to use photosynthesis to turn that energy into food?

8. The sun releases enough energy to keep green plants operating for a long time, but what's happening to the sun? In the restored "new heavens and new earth," what will be the energy source that never wears out?

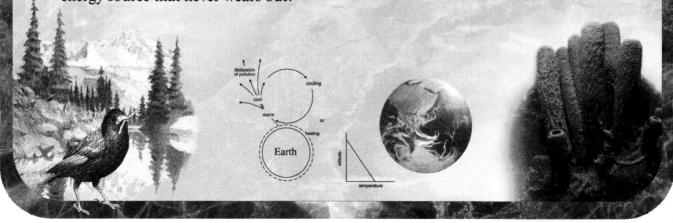

Population Balance

Food relationships and recycling are very important parts of the web of life. But God created living things to multiply and fill the earth. In our fallen world, most organisms could multiply and *overfill* the earth very quickly. What keeps living things from multiplying faster than their food supplies and mineral resources? What keeps populations in balance with their ecosystems?

Predator-prey feedback control. Most people have seen pictures of a lion pouncing on a zebra or a pack of wolves hunting down a caribou, and maybe some people have actually seen a bird catch a bug and eat it. Animals like vultures and buzzards that eat the flesh of dead animals are called **scavengers**. **Predators** are animals that hunt down other animals while they're still alive, kill them, and eat them. A predator's victim is its **prey**.

When most people think of population control in nature, they think of predators ripping up and devouring their prey. No animals got their food like that in the perfect and peaceful world God created, but several animals began to live as predators after sin entered into the world.

Predators are important parts of ecosystems today. Their role is illustrated by events that occurred in the

MYSTERIES OF LIFE

1. In two successive winters, over 60,000 deer starved in the Grand Canyon area.

2. Animal populations can be kept in check without predators.

3. The flocking of birds could be a kind of census.

Can You Provide the Explanations?

Kaibab Forest on the north rim of the Grand Canyon in the early part of this century. With the thought that the deer population of the forest was being kept too low by mountain lions, wolves, and coyotes, a massive campaign to eliminate these predators was begun. From 1907 to 1939, hundreds of mountain lions and over 7,000 coyotes were killed. By 1918, the deer population had increased from 4,000 to 40,000, and the plants in the deer's range began to show damage. The population reached 100,000 by 1923, and during the next two winters about 60,000 deer starved to death. By 1939, 10,000 deer were left on a much-damaged range. Although it would not be obvious to the deer being eaten, it is clear in this particular case that the predators were, in a sense, doing a favor for the animal population on which they preyed.

Predator control of insect populations is extremely important, and this task often falls to birds. Woodpeckers, for example, normally help to keep populations of bark beetles under control, although substances in tree sap also protect trees from the ravages of these beetles. In the White River National Forest of Colorado, a windstorm blew over several trees, weakening but not killing them. Beetles began to multiply under the bark of these weakened trees, and a later snowfall sheltered the multiplying beetles from predation by woodpeckers. By springtime, the beetle population had reached such huge numbers that woodpeckers were unable to eat them fast enough. Assaulting trees in overwhelming numbers, the beetles also overcame the natural resistance of the trees, paving the way for a real disaster. The forest was severely damaged. Since the forest served as a watershed for the plains area downstream, the effects of the bark beetle population explosion were felt by farmers and ranchers far away.

In the predator-prey relationship, most people think that it is the predator that controls the prey population, and that was the emphasis in the examples above. But, it is just as true to say that the *prey controls the predator population*. When deer are in short supply, for example, mountain lions have a much more difficult time finding and capturing them, and many of the lions starve to death or at least have fewer cubs. There is, then, a **feedback** between predator and prey populations as diagrammed below: high lion population produces low deer, which in turn produces low lion, which produces high deer, which starts the cycle over with high lion population.

The effect of prey in regulating predator populations can be seen in the effect of mass extermination of prairie dog colonies in parts of the West. The prairie dog decline brought their chief predator, the black-footed ferret, nearly to extinction. Similarly, a cyclical decrease in Canadian snowshoe hare populations forces the snowy owls that feed on them to range far south in search of food, and still the owl population declines.

In a fallen world, predator-prey interaction helps to regulate both predator and prey populations. But this control mechanism is far less important than most people suppose. Human hunters usually take strong, healthy, "trophy" specimens, but animal hunters usually kill only weaker, ailing, and aged prey, so prey populations are largely unaffected.

Note that God did NOT create predator-prey population control. The delicate balance between predator and prey populations that continues for many years may look "designed," but it is not. After man's sin when some animals began to eat others, the decline in their food supply (prey) "automatically" set limits on the killers' population and started the self-regulating feedback cycle. It was the change in animal behavior, not God's plan at creation, that gave us predator-prey balance.

But, one might be asking, if predators didn't control populations in the world God created, what did? Without predators, wouldn't

High mountain lion population

Low deer population

Low mountain lion population

High deer population

Predator-prey feedback population control. Prey populations are perhaps more effective in regulating predator populations by limiting their food supply than predators are at regulating prey, but the relationship definitely works both ways.

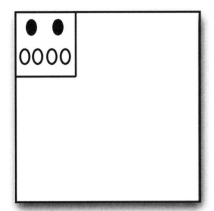

1st year
Original mating pair establish territory in woodlot for themselves and four offspring.

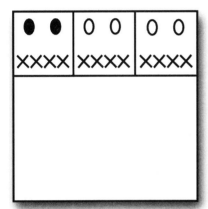

2nd year
Original pair and their offspring or equivalent again establish territories.

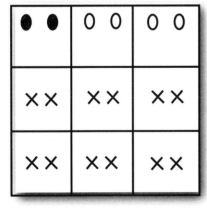

3rd year
The woodlot is now full, and no new mating pairs will be established until natural death or emigration opens up new territories.

Territorial population control, which provides a means of multiplying and filling an area without either overfilling it or struggling to the death with members of the same or a different species.

many things go beyond God's command to multiply and fill the earth, and overfill it? The answer is no, because of the *created* population control mechanism called **territoriality**.

Territorial population control. Territorial population control provides an excellent means whereby a species can multiply and fill an area without overfilling it — and without struggling to the death with members of its own or another species.

As an example of territorial population control, consider the filling of a woodlot starting with a pair of birds moving into a new territory (see diagram at left). As the birds look for nesting sites, the male searches out a territory where food supply is sufficient for him, his mate, and their future offspring. He establishes the boundaries of his territory by flying from limb to limb, chirping a warning to other males of his species that this territory has been reserved. Most people think the sweet sounds of male birds in the spring are love songs for attracting a mate, but not always. The song is often one male warning another: "Posted. No trespassing. Violators will be pecked!" (Male dogs use urine to mark their territories.)

In the incredible provision of God, birds usually assess their territorial needs quite accurately, even varying it according to prevailing climatic conditions, and only rarely are they caught by some kind of environmental disaster. Within this territory, the male and his mate are able to raise their family. Let us assume, for convenience, that they have four offspring.

The following year, the original pair migrates back to the woodlot, and reclaims the old territory. The two pairs of young, or their equivalent, stake out two territories of their own. Overcrowding is avoided because males usually respect the chirping signals that mark boundaries. In case of a dispute, two males may engage in **ritualistic combat**, which in many birds involves a singing duel, and perhaps the intense fluttering of wings. Usually the bird that first staked out the territory feels strongest about it and fights hardest, a sort of "survival of the firstest." A male's courage seems to dwindle the farther away he gets from the center of his territory. The whole system works quite nicely, and the price is only a few songs and perhaps a few ruffled feathers.

This process continues until the woodlot is fully divided up into territories for mating pairs and their families. The birds that have not been able to establish a territory do not mate that year, but wait until the emigration or death of a mating pair opens up a new space. In this way, overcrowding is avoided, and an ample food supply (barring ecological disaster) is guaranteed for all. The non-mating birds constitute a reservoir from which the species can draw, as mating pairs die or simply move away.

Cranes in ritualistic combat

Unlike predator-prey balance, territoriality is a *created* pattern. The instincts for recognizing territory and respecting ritualistic combat must be programmed into the birds ahead of time by that "Master Programmer," God himself.

Evolution based on chance mutations and a winner-take-all struggle for survival could not *produce* territorial population control, but it could easily *destroy* it. Suppose some mutant of the species lost either the instinct for territorial marking or the respect for ritualistic combat. Unfortunately, such a mutant would have survival value, crowding out and perhaps even killing off other members of its species whose instincts would make a duel to the death unthinkable. As a result of this evolutionary advantage, the combative members of a species might crowd out and even drive to extinction other members of the species. In the long run, of course, the loss of territorial population control may be disastrous for the species: it may become extinct as it overcrowds its environment, or it may become a "victim" of predator control.

God's wisdom and forethought are awesomely displayed in a form of territorial population control practiced by sea lions and albatrosses. These creatures spend their adult lives swimming or flying over vast stretches of the ocean, but annually they return to certain particular islands to breed. In the breeding areas, adults stake out a territory only a few square meters in size, which obviously has nothing to do with the feeding needs of the animals. Or does it? It actually seems that the territories marked off in the breeding areas are **symbolic territories**, representing the right to feed and hunt over a certain portion of the ocean. If there are more birds or sea lions than there are nesting areas, those that do not find a territory do not mate until a new territory opens up, or until they can drive off an older mating pair. This insures an ample food supply when the group returns to hunting and feeding in the ocean.

Again, an evolutionary mutant that lost its ability to recognize territorial limitations and

simply went off to breed on another part of the island would wreak havoc on the species, although gaining a short term advantage for himself and his descendants. In God's providence, not all species lost their created ability to multiply and fill, but not overfill, the earth.

Plants can also stake out territories. In a desert, for example, some plants are so regularly spaced that they almost look planted. In many cases, spacing results from **inhibitors** secreted by the roots of those plants that first establish themselves in an area. Other plants of that species will not be able to grow where the concentration of these inhibitors is high. The result is enough water, sun, and nutrients for each plant, which is quite important in areas like deserts, where crowding would be disastrous.

Other social means of population control. Territoriality is the most important member of a group of population control mechanisms called "social," because they are based on behavioral relationships among members of a species, quite apart from predator-prey cycles, disease, or starvation.

Flocking, the tendency of masses of birds to fly around the trees in which they are nesting, seems to give the birds a sense of their population size. Large flock size results in fewer eggs, and vice versa, thereby effecting population control.

Among arena birds, courtship displays of males take place in a specific area, the arena, and only a certain number of males are able to perform, thereby limiting population growth, and forcing some males to wait for a better year. The bowerbirds, such as the bird-of-paradise and the cock-of-the-rock, build individual courtship display areas, called bowers, often decorating them daily with fresh flowers. Some birds have iridescent and/or brightly colored feathers or inflatable neck sacs that serve in the courtship ritual, and also in ritualistic combat with other males for territories. Only those successful in courtship display

A bower bird

example, are "bathed" in abundant food in autumn, yet their population is maintained at low levels in anticipation, as it were, of the winter shortages to come.

Two things evolution can't do that God can are (1) plan ahead and (2) program systems with multiple complex interdependent parts. Territoriality and social population control clearly reflect God's wisdom and show us how God could design a world *without predators* where each species could multiply and fill its place in God's plan. Had we filled the earth without sin, what then? Mars, the Milky Way, who knows? An infinite time to explore an infinite space to learn an infinite amount about our transcendently infinite God?

acquire breeding rights, thus limiting population size in these species.

Some plants and animals release chemicals into the environment, called **pheromones**, which influence the reproductive behavior of other members of their species. Pheromones include the root secretions involved in the spacing of desert plants noted above, and sex attractants, like that which enables the male gypsy moth to find a female over a distance of miles (kilometers). The sexual maturity of some fern plants is inhibited by pheromones released by other ferns maturing earlier in the same area, preventing overcrowding at a given time. Pheromones released by slipper shell snails can change the sex of other slipper shells, resulting in a balance of sexes and also regulating the timing of fertilization.

Again, the fascinating feature of so many of these social means of population control is their allowing species to adjust population in advance of food shortages. Chickadees, for

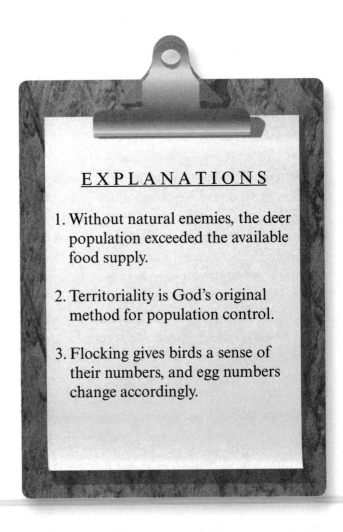

EXPLANATIONS

1. Without natural enemies, the deer population exceeded the available food supply.

2. Territoriality is God's original method for population control.

3. Flocking gives birds a sense of their numbers, and egg numbers change accordingly.

1. Animals that eat dead and decomposing flesh (like buzzards eat road kill) are called _____. Animals that capture other animals alive (prey), kill, and eat them are called _____.

2. It's all too obvious that predators control prey populations by killing and eating them, but what controls predator populations and how do they do it?

3. Diagram a predator-prey feedback cycle for coyotes and rabbits like the one in the text for mountain lions and deer.

4. Did God create predator-prey population balance? If not, then how did it get started?

5. God did create a means of population balance involving no death called _____.

6. What are some of the ways animals mark their territories? How do animals defend their territories without hurting or killing each other? Name an animal that has a "symbolic territory," a small nesting area that represents feeding rights to a vast territory.

7. Did God even give some plants a means to "multiply and fill," but not overfill, an area? Give an example.

8. Since evolutionists believe time, chance, struggle, and death made everything, they can believe predator-prey balance started without God's help. But can evolution by chance and struggle make territorial population control? Why or why not? What would "evolution," in the sense of chance and struggle, do to the territoriality God created?

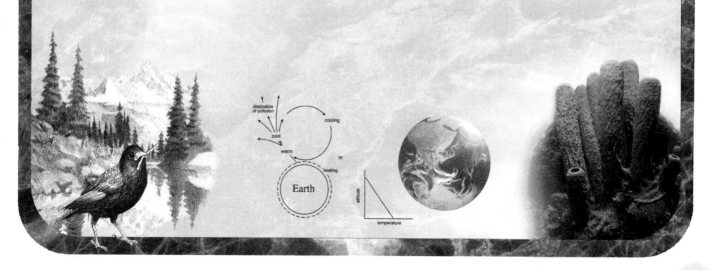

Population Growth and Control

J-shaped population cycles. Population growth in a given area can usually be represented by a **sigmoid**, or S-shaped, **growth curve**. The population starts at a low level. Then, after a **lag period**, it increases at a very rapid, logarithmic rate, the **log phase**. Finally, it levels off (*lag → log → level*) at some equilibrium population number that fluctuates only slightly from year to year. (See charts on following page.)

Animals with a **J-shaped** population growth curve undergo alternate periods of "boom and bust," building up rapidly to extremely high levels, and then dropping off to near zero before the second J-shaped curve begins. If territoriality reflects creation, J curves illustrate corruption and catastrophe.

The lemmings of Scandinavia behave in this way. These cute, furry creatures remain very active year around, feeding and breeding in their burrows under the snow, even during the cold northern winters.

After about four years of such population growth, the lemmings begin their famous mass migration toward the sea. They seem to move

MYSTERIES OF LIFE

1. Lemmings plunge into the ocean in mass numbers.

2. Many squirrels, birds, cats, and rabbits turned up dead in eastern Illinois.

3. Robins and cardinals were disappearing from backyards.

Can You Provide the Explanations?

purposefully and unhesitatingly, and when they reach the coastline, they plunge into the water rather deliberately and swim out into the Atlantic Ocean. They do not make it across, of course, and thus the total population is reduced to an extremely low level. Those left behind begin anew, however, and in another four years or so, the cycle is repeated.

The same kind of cycle is seen in the snowshoe hares of North America, although this cycle tends to run 7 to 11 years in length, rather than 4 or 5. At high population levels, the hares show evidence of extreme physiological stress. Their hormone levels are abnormal, they are very excitable, and their blood sugar is at a dangerously low level (hypoglycemia). In such a condition, the hares can be literally frightened to death (and some Canadians have used this knowledge to prepare rabbit stew without having to pick out the buckshot). The large majority dies when this point in the cycle is reached, reducing the population suddenly to very low levels. This has catastrophic effects as well on the predators of the snowshoe hares, which may be driven far from their normal ranges in search for food.

Why these animals undergo such sudden population changes is not yet known. Although snowshoe hares show evidence of physiological stress, lemmings do not. It is interesting that laboratory animals forced into over-crowded situations frequently develop nervous and hormonal disorders, and begin to behave in erratic and even self-destructive ways. Some think that human beings subjected to severe overcrowding will also develop behavior abnormalities. Evidence can be cited both for and against this thesis. Behavior of overcrowded rats becomes atrocious. Yet in a world that is clearly crowded in many places, it may be comforting to know that a very densely populated country, Holland, is also world famous for its very personal hospitality and friendliness.

Artificial means of population control. Many times man has tried to regulate the population of some other species, especially crop pests. The two most common means are chemical control and biological control. **Chemical control** is illustrated by the use of *pesticides* and *herbicides* in the control of insects and weeds.

In recent years, chemical control mechanisms have come under heavy fire, and they have been responsible for some ecological disasters or near-disasters. For example, a portion of eastern Illinois was sprayed with chlorinated hydrocarbons in an attempt to block westward expansion of the Japanese beetle. The spray failed to block the beetle's progress, but nearly eradicated many bird species, ground squirrels, and farm cats, and killed or poisoned many sheep, muskrat, and rabbits. DDT buildup in fat tissue has resulted in massive fish kills and produced thin eggshells in several bird species. DDT has already reached a concentration of 12 ppm (parts per million) in the fat tissues of the average American, a level that would render a

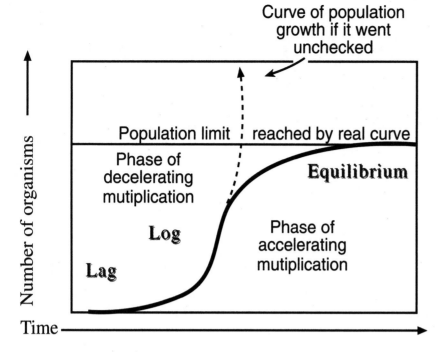

Curve of population growth if it went unchecked

Population limit ¦ reached by real curve

Phase of decelerating mutiplication

Equilibrium

Log

Phase of accelerating mutiplication

Lag

Number of organisms

Time

These charts show the contrast between the more common sigmoid or S-shaped population growth curve and the J-shaped "boom or bust" curve of the snowshoe hare and its predator, the lynx.

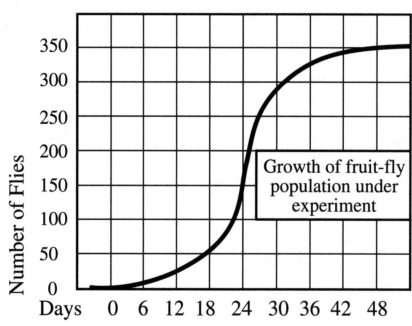

Growth of fruit-fly population under experiment

Number of Flies

Days

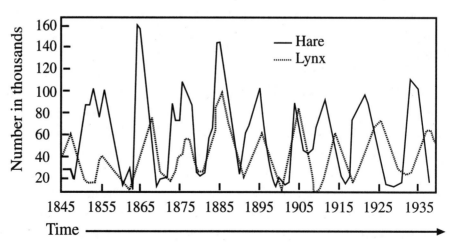

Number in thousands

—— Hare
.... Lynx

Time

meat animal unfit for consumption. In Peru, a valley's cotton production was first increased by DDT, but then decreased four years later, because predators of pests suffered more than the pests themselves and could not recover as well.

One must recognize that chemicals such as DDT have made the quality of life much higher for many peoples around the world at least in short-range terms, but as chlorinated hydrocarbons and other long lasting and non-specific poisons build up on the biosphere, a search for alternatives is necessary.

Biological control is the introduction of predators or specific disease organisms to control an undesirable population. After a massive shooting campaign failed, viruses were used with relative success to control the population of imported rabbits in Australia. Ladybird beetles have long been used successfully to control scale insects in the orchards of California.

The use of radiation-sterilized males successfully eliminated the screwworm fly from Florida, without having any adverse effects on other species or any pesticide carry-over problems. Traps using gyplure, the sex attractant of the gypsy moth, have been successful in controlling the population of this species whose caterpillar can be quite destructive to forest trees.

But biological control has its problems, too. The starling was originally imported from England to control the elm spanworm in New York City's Central Park. The starling did a great job there, but then continued to multiply

Crop dusting with airplanes is one method of chemical pest control.

across the continent, displacing more desirable species (including chasing friendly robins and cardinals from people's backyards). English sparrows have a similar history in the United States.

At this stage of the earth's history, man cannot simply give up the attempt to regulate some populations. Crop pests are a serious hazard, not only to us, but sometimes to other species as well. Furthermore, the way people move around the globe sooner or later introduces new species into foreign areas, sometimes creating problems that, since they are of our own making, we ought to solve. These comments on chemical and biological control, however, point out that the task is a most difficult and demanding one, requiring not only much knowledge but also a good measure of wisdom and a real sense of stewardship.

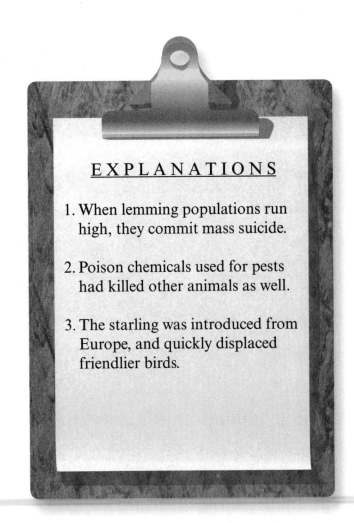

EXPLANATIONS

1. When lemming populations run high, they commit mass suicide.

2. Poison chemicals used for pests had killed other animals as well.

3. The starling was introduced from Europe, and quickly displaced friendlier birds.

1. Diagram a sigmoid (S-shaped) growth curve, and label *lag*, *log*, and *level* phases.

2. Name an animal with J-shaped, "boom-and-bust" population cycles. Is that population in or out of control?

3. Give an example of an artificial *chemical* control of populations. Give an example of an artificial *biological* control.

4. Give an example of a:
   a. problem with chemical control
   b. problem with biological control
   c. success with biological control

Succession

In the food relationships and population control mechanisms described earlier, we have seen how biotic communities can maintain the same balance year after year. But communities also change in response to changing conditions, and they initiate changes either by colonizing new areas or by reclaiming areas that were damaged or destroyed by wind, water, or fire. As one community moves into an area, it changes the environment and paves the way for the succeeding community. This process, and the resulting sequence of community changes, is called **succession.**

The first group of plants and animals to move into an area is called the **pioneer** community, while the last community, which is capable of maintaining itself indefinitely, is called the **climax**. Intermediate communities are called **seral stages**, and a complete sequence from pioneer through intermediate to climax communities is called a **sere**. Some examples will help make these concepts clear and help to indicate the significance of succession.

Bare rock succession. Perhaps the most challenging environment which living things can invade is a bare rock environment, where living things must gain a foothold in barren

---

MYSTERIES OF LIFE

1. Plants, as well as animals, migrate.

2. Alligator and palm tree fossils have been found at the North Pole.

3. There was no rain on the earth in its earliest days.

Can You Provide the Explanations?

Lichen growing on rock

to enter the succession. The shrub stage paves the way for the *forest* climax stage, if climatic conditions are suitable, by further anchoring the soil, providing shade and increased moisture-holding capacity, by reducing the effects of wind, etc.

A bare rock-to-forest sere can often be seen along a road cut through a rocky hill or along a creek bank (see illustration on following page).

Lichens can be seen growing on the rock, mosses in pockets of shallow soil, ferns in various cracks and crevices in the rock where soil accumulates, shrubs and trees further back where the rocks have been covered over with the buildup of soil, and roots have penetrated into crevices. Depending on a variety of conditions and the rock type, bare rock succession can take

mineral surroundings. These conditions may have prevailed over a large part of the earth following creation, and again following the Flood. On a smaller scale, such conditions may follow a volcanic lava or ash flow, severe flood, or fire.

About the only forms of life that grow on bare rock are **lichens**. These incredible "combination plants" include green algae that absorb moisture and carbon dioxide from the air for photosynthesis, and they also have fungal elements that secrete acids capable of dissolving rocks and absorbing water and minerals. Lichens, then, are exquisitely designed to be the pioneer community in bare rock succession.

As the lichens continue to grow, they form soil from the dissolved minerals mixed with their decayed remains. In this thin film of soil, *moss* spores can germinate and grow. The mosses, in turn, provide a depth of soil and moisture-holding capacity that is capable of supporting a growth of *ferns* or similar plants. The underground stems of ferns hold the increasing depth of soil in place and make it possible for *shrubs*

decades, centuries, or perhaps a thousand years. The final climax, of course, will vary depending on the biome in which the succession occurs.

The preceding example shows that plants lead the way in ecological succession. A succession of animal communities follows the changes in plants and, of course, contributes to modifying the environment. In the environment provided by lichens, a few *protozoans* can grow. In the moss stage, *worms* are present. With ferns we find some *insects*, with shrubs we find *birds* and with trees, generally speaking, we find various kinds of *mammals*.

<u>Succession versus evolution.</u> In many ways the *observable* process of succession parallels the *hypothetical* process of evolution. In both cases, relatively simple plant and animal communities come first, and are followed by more complex and increasingly diversified flora and fauna (plants and animals).

There are, however, two radical differ-

Bare rock succession

ences between the *real* process of succession and the *imagined* process of evolution. First, evolutionists demand that evolution takes millions and billions of years, while succession takes place in a few tens of years, perhaps centuries, or at most a thousand years. Second, succession involves only migration, not mutation. In evolutionary theory, it is presumed that protozoans evolved into worms, which evolved into insects, for example. In succession, all of these forms of life exist simultaneously in different areas of the earth, and they only migrate into a certain area as conditions become favorable. Plants, of course, "migrate" by shedding spores and seeds, which travel wide distances, but only develop when conditions become suitable.

Some species thrive under a wide variety of ecological conditions, and so are found in different ecosystems and seral stages. Such species are called **eury-** with a suffix that tells what broad variation they can tolerate. Species that do well with lots of variation in temperature or salt, for example, are called **eurythermal** and **euryhaline**, respectively.

Species that can live only within a narrow range of some environmental factor are called **steno-**, like **stenothermal** or **stenohaline**. Species that are restricted to one ecosystem or one seral stage are called **index species**. The red-backed

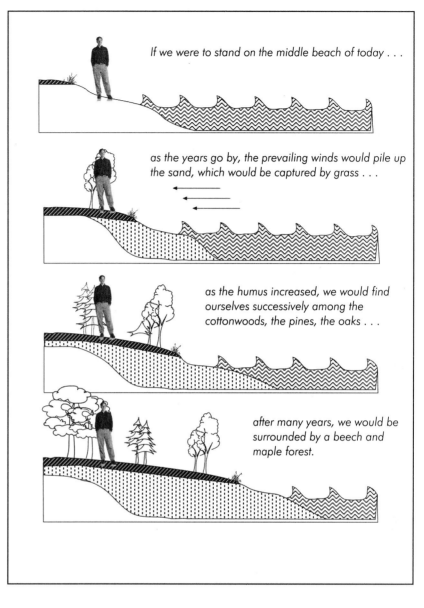

If we were to stand on the middle beach of today . . .

as the years go by, the prevailing winds would pile up the sand, which would be captured by grass . . .

as the humus increased, we would find ourselves successively among the cottonwoods, the pines, the oaks . . .

after many years, we would be surrounded by a beech and maple forest.

 Sand — at the time we first sat on the middle beach.

 Sand — washed up by the waves and blown by the wind, since we first sat on the beach.

Humus — added by plants and animals.

Sand dune succession at the classic site, the southern end of Lake Michigan.

salamander, for example, can live only in a beech-maple forest, so it's an **index** of the beech-maple climax community. So-called *index fossils* may be index species to pre-Flood environments.

Succession as an ecological process has only been understood scientifically in the last

Bog lake filling

Lake

Fill

Bedrock

Pond succession in the Canadian taiga.

century. The classic study was done on sand dune succession in Indiana at the southern tip of Lake Michigan. As sand from the lake currents is washed up on the southern shores, it is colonized and stabilized by a series of plant communities: first the pioneer grasses, then the sun-tolerant trees like chokecherries and cottonwoods, which are followed by a series of increasingly shade-tolerant trees, such as pines, oaks, and finally, the beech-maple climax. Characteristic animals are found in each stage, such as the white tiger beetle with the beach grass and cottonwoods, the bronze tiger beetle in the pine stage, and the green tiger beetle and red-backed salamander in the beech-maple climax.

Occasionally a strong wind will produce a "blowout" in a sand dune area, uprooting trees and plants and freeing the sand so that it moves as dunes again. After a blowout, or a fire or flood, succession in that area must start over at an earlier stage.

Aquatic succession. The filling in of lakes and ponds is one of the most familiar examples of succession, and the process can be a real nuisance to farmers and fishermen who want to keep a pond at a relatively early successional stage.

Consider a pond formed by a dam, either natural or manmade, along a small creek. Silt, leaf litter, and the remains of organisms gradually build up in the pond. From the edges, emergent, submerged, and floating vegetation gradually move toward the center of the pond. Fish that need much open water, such as bass or trout, are replaced by herbivorous fish, such as carp, much to the distaste of fishermen, swimmers, and boaters. The colonizers come from nearby environments where they are already established, animals wandering in search of food, seeds and spores blowing in the wind, sticky fish eggs "hitchhiking" on birds' legs, etc.

The natural process of lake and pond filling is called **eutrophication**. This term has become popular in magazines and newspapers, because pollutants such as nitrates and phosphates, which are natural fertilizers, tend to speed up eutrophication, rapidly filling some well-known lakes.

The events of pond succession as they occur in the spruce forest of Canada are exquisitely recorded in a prize-winning film, *The Spruce Bog*. The succession starts when a beaver dam or rockslide causes a stream to back up, beginning the *open-water* phase. Because of low average temperatures in this biome, decomposition is slow, and the non-porous soil layer underneath traps the products of decomposition, turning the water acid. *Sphagnum moss* is the only plant that can grow luxuriantly in such acid waters. This moss begins to grow in from the edge, gradually choking off the open water.

At the descriptively named "quaking bog" stage, the mossy mat itself forms a somewhat shaky base for a succession of other plants and their accompanying animal communities. Labrador tea and bog cranberry are among the early plants, as well as the insect-trapping pitcher plant. At this stage, the bog provides a home for such waterfowl as the loon. As the moss gets denser, woody shrubs become dominant, finally giving way to the climax forest of tamarack or larch and the predominant black spruce. These trees provide a home for the spruce grouse and other animals, and shade for such plants as the delicate lady slipper orchid. After perhaps a thousand years of succession, slowed down by the low temperatures of this region, the forest has replaced the spruce bog completely.

Succession may be studied on a more manageable time scale by observing the changes that occur in laboratory cultures of microbes. A **hay infusion** is a water sample including some hay to which microbial spores and cysts are normally attached. It passes through several successional stages within a few weeks. The bacteria are the first to appear, and they provide food for protozoans. The protozoans, in turn, provide food for each other in an orderly sequence of events that moves through particular stages to a climax community.

New growth

<u>Secondary succession.</u> The above are all examples of **primary succession**, i.e., they begin where little or no life exists in a given area at the start. **Secondary succession** begins with good soil or with some relatively complex community already in existence. A common example of secondary succession is **"old field" succession**, the gradual overgrowth by surrounding plants and animals of an abandoned field once used for farming. The grasses give way to flowering weeds and the small, sun-tolerant trees appear. Years later, the climax shade-tolerant trees begin growing up under the earlier trees that had paved the way for their succession.

Secondary succession may be observed locally in a yard or vacant lot left unmowed. Knowing the area and the natural vegetation common to that area, it is fairly easy to predict what weeds, shrubs, and trees will move in, when, and in what order. Because it starts with conditions already quite suitable for a complex community, secondary succession can occur quite rapidly. Many were surprised at how fast Yellowstone National Park recovered from a colossal fire, and coral reefs can recover from boat damage quickly from one year to the next.

To a man mowing a yard, clearing a field for cultivation, or maintaining a pond suitable for bass fishing, succession can appear to be an enemy. Normally, however, succession develops the most life for an area, in accord with the climate.

Succession might be called "ecological growth." A baby starts as a single cell, a cell with a plan for development built in by God. Thanks to God's pre-planning, arms, legs, eyes, and ears appear in an orderly sequence, and new skills and abilities develop as that one cell gives way to many specialized ones — muscle, nerve, skin, etc. Succession is like that: from simple beginnings plus God's plan, more and more complex and varied ecosystems "grow" over the earth.

Since God created plants and animals to multiply and fill the earth, there must have been open areas at the end of the creation week, ready to be filled by primary ecological succession. After Noah's flood, succession began again, with secondary succession rapidly filling some areas following that awesome catastrophe. Succession also brings "healing" to damaged ecosystems, a foretaste of the great healing to come with Christ's return.

Earth's Environment Before and After Noah's Flood. Although the earth is still a wonderful and fascinating place in many ways, it is certainly no longer a garden of peaceful perfection (Eden). Scripture and science suggest the earth's environment was also changed in dramatic ways by Noah's flood.

Fossils of alligators and palm trees are found near both North and South Poles. That and similar evidences suggest to many scientists that the earth once had a mild climate from "top to bottom" and lacked vast stretches of either ice or desert. Furthermore, the atmosphere today contains only 0.03 percent CO_2, yet green plants grow best with over ten times as much, 0.5 percent, an amount sometimes used to produce luxuriant growth in greenhouses.

It really seems that God designed the world originally with much more CO_2. That "greenhouse gas" would have helped give the world a milder pole-to-pole climate — although there would still be cooler places at higher altitudes and latitudes, and ecological variation based on differences in moisture, day length, and soil type. The extra CO_2 would also stimulate plant growth, help dissolve minerals, and perhaps influence breathing and circulation in animals and people. At the time of the Flood, much of the CO_2 would be buried as coal, oil, natural gas, and fossil-bearing limestone rock, unavailable for immediate recirculation to the atmosphere, leaving green plants "gasping for breath," as it were.

Reduction of that greenhouse gas would also be like throwing the blanket off on a cold night. Land cools much more quickly than water, setting the stage for moisture evaporated from warm oceans to fall on continents as snow at higher altitudes and latitudes, helping to produce the so-called Ice Age that began after the Flood and continues to a lesser extent today. (Thirty percent of the continents were once covered with ice; 10 percent are still covered.)

Some scientists and Bible scholars believe there was no rain before the Flood, but that "a mist went up to water the face of the ground" (Gen. 2:6). An underground watering system bringing minerals up to plant roots (instead of washing them away, as rain can do) could produce hardier, more nutritious vegetation. The nutritional value of plants would also be affected by the change in soils from those based on weathered, created rock to those based on post-Flood fossil-bearing sedimentary rock. The decline in plant and soil conditions following the Flood may have been among the reasons God said to Noah as he left the ark, "As I gave you the green plants to eat, so now you may eat meat" (Gen. 9:3). The decline in both the quantity and quality of plant foods following the Flood (plus perhaps the carcasses available and fish trapped in drying ponds) may also have triggered a spurt of change from plant-eating to meat-eating, and an increase of self-developing predator-prey population balance over the "kinder, gentler" instinctive territorial control.

Some say, using both science and the Bible, that the earth once had a transparent water vapor canopy around it. Such a canopy would contribute to the beneficial greenhouse effect. It could also produce the health benefits of shielding us from some radiation and of doubling atmosphere oxygen pressure. These, in turn, might help us explain how pre-Flood peoples lived so long (into the 900s) and why so many plants and animals have fossil forms so much bigger than similar ones living today.

Earth is still a wonderful home, but the roof leaks, some windows are broken, there are too many roaches, and some of the garden soil has washed away.

We need to keep the best and repair the rest! Praise God, when Jesus returns we get a new and permanent home even better than before!

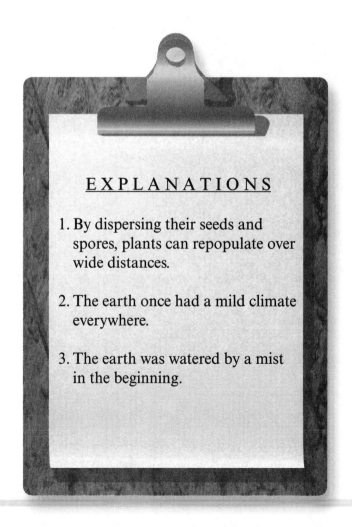

EXPLANATIONS

1. By dispersing their seeds and spores, plants can repopulate over wide distances.

2. The earth once had a mild climate everywhere.

3. The earth was watered by a mist in the beginning.

1. An orderly sequence of change in which one community changes the environment and paves the way for a succeeding community is called _____.

2. In ecological succession, the first stage is called the _____, the final stage (which can continue to reproduce itself) is the _____, and the in-between communities are called _____ stages.

3. The algal-fungal pioneers in bare rock succession that can dissolve rock and build soil are called _____.

4. Arrange these alphabetized plants in bare rock succession to show the increase in soil depth, shade, and moisture-holding capacity: ferns, lichens, mosses, shrubs, and trees. (Diagram with arrows.)

5. Arrange these alphabetized animals as they follow plants in bare rock succession: birds, insects, mammals, protozoans, and worms. (Diagram with arrows.)

6. Succession is a real process that changes an area with a few simple life forms into one with many complex forms. Give two major ways succession is TOTALLY DIFFERENT from the imaginary simple-to-complex series called evolution.

7. A sea snail that can live in only a narrow range of saltiness is called _____-haline (eury-, steno-), and it might be a good _____ (index, appendix) species for a certain ecosystem.

8. Beach grasses and a series of sun-tolerant then shade-tolerant trees anchor the sand, build soil, and produce shade in _____ succession.

9. What kind of succession has the special name "eutrophication"?

10. "Old field succession," replacement of an abandoned farmer's field by a predictable series of weeds and trees, is an example of _____ (primary, secondary) succession that occurs _____ (fast, slowly) because it starts with rich soil, _____ (like, unlike) the succession that occurred after Noah's flood.

11. Noah's flood probably made big changes in the earth's ecology. Mark the following as likely "BF" (before flood), "AF" (after flood), or "BA" (before and after):
    a. __ warm, mild climate pole to pole
    b. __ ice sheets and glaciers
    c. __ rain leaching minerals away from plant roots
    d. __ springs bringing minerals up to plant roots, and mist to water plants
    e. __ higher CO_2 levels and more abundant plant growth
    f. __ man allowed by God to eat meat
    g. __ seasons marked by photoperiod (day length variation)

UNIT FOUR:

THE INDIVIDUAL AND THE SPECIES IN THE ECOSYSTEM

We started our journey by looking at the whole earth, then we looked at the biomes, then the communities. We have narrowed our focus each time. We will continue to do so in this unit, looking at individual species and how they adapt to their surroundings. Get ready to find out about some bizarre and interesting creatures — like the bold Egyptian plover, honeybees, farmer ants, woodpeckers, remora fish, and flukes.

Niches, Habitats, and Adaptations

T he central theme in ecology is that no individual or species exists by itself. Each is part of the total web of life, interacting with many other living things and with its physical environment.

Niche refers to an organism's occupation, or the things it does in its ecosystem. Consider squirrels, for example. Squirrels make nests in hollow trees and in branches of trees. They collect nuts and seeds, serving both to distribute the seeds for plants and to provide themselves as well as other organisms with food stores for the winter. Squirrels fall prey to other animals; they are host to a variety of parasites; and they transmit or act as reservoirs for a variety of diseases. The rustling of squirrels through trees may alert other animals to the approach of man and other dangers. All of these things are part of the niche of the squirrel. As can be seen, the sudden disappearance of squirrels from a given area would have diverse effects on a variety of plants and other animals. To a greater or lesser degree, the same is true of all other species.

Trees have particularly broad niches. A

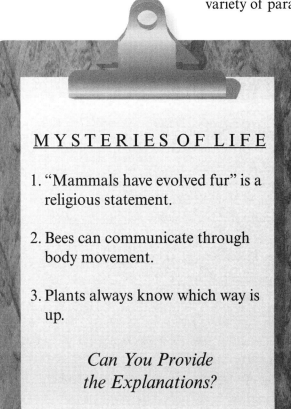

MYSTERIES OF LIFE

1. "Mammals have evolved fur" is a religious statement.

2. Bees can communicate through body movement.

3. Plants always know which way is up.

Can You Provide the Explanations?

tree provides food and shelter for a wide variety of animals: fruits for some animals, sap for others, leaf litter for still others, homes in its branches for some, within its trunk for others, and under its leaves for still others. Trees anchor the soil in place, add humus to the soil, shelter it from the erosional effects of wind and water, and shield it from the drying rays of the sun. Trees break the wind and moderate its chilling effects. The niche of a typical tree is broad indeed.

Some species are, of course, ecologically more important than others. A blight that wipes out the dominant trees in an area will have a greater effect on the overall ecology than the demise of one species of spider, for example. But no strand in the web of life can break without some effect on the whole.

Habitat refers to an organism's address, the place where it lives. The general habitat is described in terms of such factors as temperature, sunlight, moisture, soil and mineral factors, wind, altitude, latitude, salinity and current in aquatic ecosystems, population density, etc. General habitat conditions are important in the distribution of many larger plants and animals,

Water strider

but smaller creatures often live under a much more restricted set of conditions called the **microhabitat**.

Some species of mosses and algae, for example, usually only grow on the north sides of certain kinds of trees, where humidity and sunlight conditions are consistently different from those on the south side of the same tree (a fact hikers can use to help determine direction). Some organisms spend their entire lives within rotting logs, where sunlight may never penetrate, the wind never blow, and the rain never fall as it does in the habitat surrounding the log. Some aquatic organisms, such as water striders or water boatman, live most of their lives on the water's surface film, a wide but very thin microhabitat.

Adaptation can be a very confusing term. Evolutionists often use it to mean the supposed process whereby organisms become better suited to their surroundings. They may say, for example, that mammals have *evolved* fur to help maintain their body heat. Creationists use adaptation to indicate how God has created

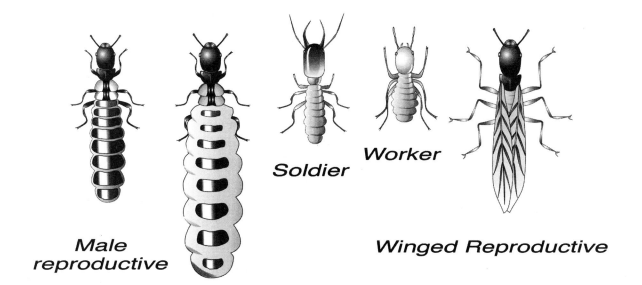

Male reproductive

Female reproductive

Soldier

Worker

Winged Reproductive

each organism with features that suit it for its purpose in God's plan. They may say, for example, that mammals have been *created* with fur to help maintain their body heat.

What is the correct scientific statement? Since science is based on repeatable public observation, the only correct scientific statement is simply "mammals *have* fur." "Mammals have *evolved* fur" is a religious statement, not a scientific one. It expresses a *faith* about what the facts of science mean, and reflects a person's choice to *worship* Mother Nature. "Mammals have been *created* with fur" likewise expresses a *faith* about the facts of science, and is a choice to *worship* the Creator rather than the creature (Rom. 1:25).

Many adaptations depend on multiple complex parts all working together in harmony at the same time. It's no wonder that Charles Darwin called adaptations "difficulties" with the theory of evolution, and called explaining the human eye through evolution by natural selection "absurd in the highest degree." In their books on ecology and other sciences, many writers freely and enthusiastically express their worship of nature. This book honors God as the One who designed each individual and species with special adaptations to suit it for its special place in His plan. *Scientifically, **adaptations** are simply features that suit an organism or species for its niche and habitat, i.e., its role and place in the web of life.*

The organism most often used to illustrate adaptations is that common but marvelous little creature, the honeybee, *Apis mellifera*. For gathering pollen, the honeybee is equipped *structurally* with pollen combs on its front legs and pollen baskets on its rear legs, both with suitable bristles. A joint in the front legs provides an antenna cleaner for wiping excess pollen from the antennae. *Functionally*, the honeybee is equipped to turn pollen and nectar into bee bread, honey, and royal jelly, all very nutritious foods that can be fed to their larvae in different doses and cause them to develop into different kinds of bees, either workers or queens. *Behaviorally*, bees are equipped with an instinctive communication system in the form of round and waggle dances that enable a scout bee to tell other bees at the hive the distance and direction to an abundant food source. These bees, using their remarkable navigation system, are able to make a "bee line" to the source.

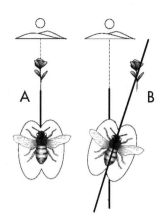

Waggle dance of the honeybee. To communicate the location of the food source to its hivemates, the common honeybee dances on the vertical surface of the hive inside the nest (A, B). If the food source lies on a straight line from hive to horizon directly below the sun, then the straight-run portion of its dance will be vertical (A). But if the food source is not on that line, then the straight run is performed at an angle to the vertical that equals the angle between the hive-to-sun line and hive-to-food line.

Bees also show *social* adaptations, having different body forms for different **social castes**: the sterile female **workers**, the male **drones**, and the **queens**. The workers are equipped for gathering honey; the queen is specialized for laying enormous numbers of eggs; and drones exist only to fertilize the queen, after which they are driven out by the other members of the hive. The society cooperates in a variety of enterprises, such as taking turns fanning the hive to provide air conditioning on hot summer days.

The honeybee illustrates four kinds of adaptations: **structural**, **functional**, **behavioral**, and **social**. Let's look at other examples of these four now, then add a fifth.

Structural adaptations. The features of the honeybee legs which are used in collecting pollen are examples of structural adaptations, or structures that suit it for a particular niche in its ecosystem. The hook-and-eyelet arrangement of barbs and barbules in feathers are among the bird's structural adaptations for flight. The woodpecker has an amazing set of structural adaptations related to its unique feeding habits.

It has four toes, two pointing up and two down, that, with the help of its short, stiff tail feathers, enable it to brace firmly on a vertical tree trunk. It has a jackhammer tough beak for drilling through wood, with suitably designed shock absorbing muscle, bone, and connective tissue around its skull to keep the bird from knocking itself silly. And, for probing the holes it drills for insects, it has a sticky tongue that is so long that it is wrapped around the head in a sheath that opens through the right nostril when in use!

Plants have a multitude of marvelous adaptations. The hinge or hammer orchid has a petal that looks like the abdomen of a female wasp. When a male wasp lands, his weight trips the hinge, and WHAM! — water pressure changes hammer the male wasp into the flower and cover him with pollen. A little dazed but perhaps not too unhappy, the wasp takes off, carrying a free load of pollen to the next orchid.

The coordinated set of drilling adaptations in the woodpecker.

<u>Functional adaptations.</u> Physiology is the study of body functions, and functional adaptations are features of physiology that suit an organism for its special place in God's plan.

A bombardier beetle is a tiny creature equipped with some "heavy artillery." At the beetle's rear are twin "cannons" loaded with explosive chemicals. If a frog or toad sneaks up looking for lunch, the beetle can inject a trigger, and BOOM! — off goes an explosion sending hot gases into the mouth of the would-be beetle eater. Now that doesn't kill the beetle eater, but it surely kills his taste for that beetle! Evolutionists have a hard time trying to explain adaptations like the bombardier beetle's, since one mistake in their trial-and-error process and BOOM! — the "evolving beetle" could blow itself to extinction!

Christians may wonder, however, why God would create such an elaborate defense mechanism if there were no animals killing others in the originally perfect world. For one thing, the beetle also uses its spray simply to mark where it has laid eggs, so other creatures won't accidentally dig them up. Remember the teeth described earlier that can be used for ripping and slashing into either fruit or flesh? Features God designed for one purpose in His perfect creation may have taken on other functions in our fallen world. Even evolutionists refer to new functions for previous features as **pre-adaptation**. With God, of course, the "planning ahead" can be deliberate.

But God told Adam after his sin that the ground would bring forth thorns and thistles (Gen. 3:18). So it is also possible that God, unwilling to leave innocent creatures at the mercy of sinful man and a fallen creation, created or activated defensive mechanisms at that time.

Physiological adaptations in plants include fantastic hormones, **auxins**, that God designed to direct growth movements called **tropisms**. Auxins accumulating on the shady side of a stem tip cause that side to grow faster, curving the stem until it is growing toward light (*positive phototropism*). Auxins accumulating on the down side of a growing root tip inhibit growth on that side, curving the root until it is growing down (*negative geotropism*). Working in cooperation with different receptors in different parts of plants, auxins also guide roots in their "search" for water (*hydrotropism*). The response to touch (*thigmotropism*) enables some plants to "climb" as tendrils wrap themselves around twigs, fences, rocks, arbors, etc.

<u>Behavioral adaptations.</u> Behavioral adaptations are those, like the dances of the bee, that involve responses of the whole organism. In the waggle or figure-eight dance of the bee (illustrated on the previous page), the angle from the vertical in the transverse portion of the dance indicates the direction toward the food source with respect to the angle of the sun, and continuous adjustment is made for the sun's constantly changing position. The number of abdominal waggles through the transverse portion of the dance and the rhythm of the dance indicate distance to the food source and how much there is. Such an adaptation is amazing enough itself, but it actually calls for an equally amazing ability on the part of the

other bees to respond to the dance and to fly out to the food source thus identified — all the while correcting for movement of the sun! Wow!

Such complex patterns of behavior that involve no prior learning are called **instincts**. Some instincts are elicited by particular stimuli called *releasers*. The red breast of its parent — or a properly colored cotton ball, for example — will release feeding behavior in young robins. Mating and courtship rituals discussed earlier are other examples of instinctive behavior.

A fascinating study of instincts and animal behavior is provided in highly readable form by Konrad Lorenz in the book *King Solomon's Ring*. Among many other things, Lorenz discusses **imprinting**, a process by which certain birds within a definite period after hatching fix themselves on a particular mobile object as their mother. Lorenz was able to train young geese to regard himself as their mother. Occasionally he could be seen scooting around the lawn of his home in Austria, quacking and being followed by a chain of little goslings. When the animals were larger, they sometimes followed in V-formation behind his bicycle!

<u>Social adaptations.</u> Sometimes species are adapted to their environment not by features shared among most of its members, but by social relationships among species members with different adaptations or different social rank. Again, honeybees illustrate this concept, with their division into three major castes: workers, drones, and queens. Only the queen can lay eggs, but she must be fed by the workers who are females unable to reproduce. The queen's ability to reproduce also involves fertilization by the males, or drones. Representatives of all these castes, then, are necessary for the full description of the niche of the honeybee. Other creatures with social castes are wasps, termites, and army ants.

Among mammals, hunting packs, such as those formed by wolves, represent social adaptations. Cooperation among members of the wolf pack makes them successful and feared hunters. Despite their ferocity, wolves also have social adaptations that tend to prevent their harming one another. When wolves get in fights with each other over food or a mate, it is rarely a fight to the death. When one animal feels itself beaten, it will suddenly turn up its neck, making itself vulnerable to instant death by a snap at the neck from the other wolf. An instinctive mechanism in the "top dog," however, seems to force it not to press its advantage, somewhat like the hero of many sword fights in the movies is unable to stab the defenseless villain. As long as the "underdog" remains in a submissive position, he is safe from harm, and the differences between the battling wolves are usually soon forgotten.

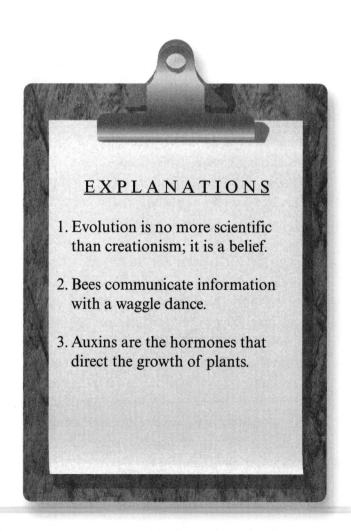

EXPLANATIONS

1. Evolution is no more scientific than creationism; it is a belief.

2. Bees communicate information with a waggle dance.

3. Auxins are the hormones that direct the growth of plants.

1. An organism's occupation, or role in its ecosystem, is called its _____; the place where it lives is called its _____.

2. The text described the niche of a squirrel and a tree. What do you think would be included in the niche of a woodpecker?

3. A forest is a habitat. A rotting log in the forest, where some insects spend all their lives, is a special, very restricted _____-habitat.

4. Features that suit living things for their roles in their ecosystems are called _____.

5. Adaptations were produced by time, chance, struggle, and death — according to a belief called _____. According to the Bible, adaptations were produced by plan, purpose, and special acts of _____. The fact that many adaptations require many parts working together at the same time supports _____ (evolution, creation).

6. Give one example from a honeybee and one from another creature to illustrate each of the four major types of adaptations:
   a. structural
   b. functional
   c. behavioral
   d. social

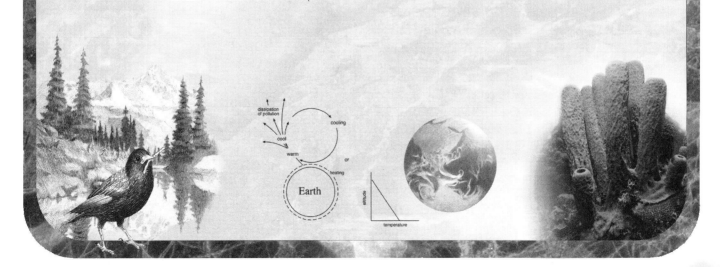

Symbiosis

Symbiosis might be called a "compound adaptation" since it involves at least two species in particularly close interdependence.

Practically beyond belief are the cleaning stations established by certain fish and shrimp at particular locations in the oceans. Large fish periodically come from miles around to these cleaning stations, advertised by the bright colors of the cleaning fish. At the cleaning stations, ferocious fish like barracudas, fresh from chasing and eating other smaller fish, passively open their mouths and let the little cleaning fish and shrimp crawl into their mouths, pick off debris and parasites, wander around among their gills, and then wander away, unharmed. Presumably, a fish that permitted this cleaning and then ate the cleaner fish would have the benefit of both clean teeth and a free meal! Such might lead to short-term evolutionary advantage, but it would break down the long-term benefit of this obviously created biotic relationship called **cleaning symbiosis**.

Cleaning symbiosis also occurs among land animals. Tickbirds feed on the hides of rhinoceroses, getting protection as well as food, and the nearly blind rhinoceros receives not only a cleaning but also is alerted to danger when the tickbird flutters away. One daring cleaner is the Egyptian plover, a bird that

MYSTERIES OF LIFE

1. Crocodiles have birds to clean their teeth.

2. Farmer ants get milk from their livestock.

3. Some human bodies are used as nesting areas for other organisms.

Can You Provide the Explanations?

walks into the open mouth of a crocodile to pick parasites from between its teeth. Even though the process probably hurts, the crocodile keeps its mouth open and, most remarkably, lets the plover walk out again, instead of receiving a free meal in addition to clean teeth.

Cleaning symbiosis is an example of **mutualism**, one of three types of symbiotic relationships.

<u>Mutualism.</u> Mutualism is a "++" symbiotic relationship, which means that both partners benefit. An intriguing example of mutualism is provided by the *yucca moth* and the *yucca plant* (illustrated below). These two species depend on each other so completely that scarcely any specimens of one exist outside the range of the other. The yucca plant, Arizona's state flower, consists of a cluster of sharp-pointed leaves around the base of a tall stalk supporting beautiful flowers. The flower is so constructed that it cannot fertilize itself.

A yucca moth, however, will crawl down into the bowl of petals, brush off some yucca pollen, roll the pollen into a ball, and place the ball of pollen under its "chin." Thus laden, it leaves the petal bowl, crawls down the outside of the flower, drills a hole through the side of the ovary and inserts the ball of pollen, thus making fertilization within the yucca possible. Then the yucca moth turns around, inserts its abdomen, and deposits *a few* of its eggs.

Rhinoceros with tickbirds

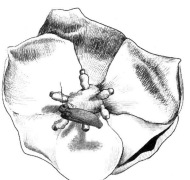

The eggs hatch into larvae or caterpillars that can only feed on yucca seeds. The larvae do not eat all the seeds, however, leaving many to propagate the yucca plant. (And how did the moth know where to find the ovary of the pistil, the seed chamber? Most college students wouldn't know where it is!)

The yucca plant/yucca moth relationship definitely meets the criteria for a created biotic relationship. Certainly mutation-selection could never begin to explain the process. Evolutionists must begin by assuming that the yucca plant or its ancestor was once able to propagate without the moth, and that the yucca moth once had other food sources. If this were correct, then natural selection would seem to prohibit the development of the kind of restrictive relationship observed. Furthermore, it seems inconceivable that any random series of mutations could produce the complicated chain of behavior actually observed in the yucca moth, especially since none of the parts of the chain would have any independent survival value. The kind of relationship observed implies the existence of an external creative agent, namely God himself!

Farmer ants provide another fascinating example of mutualism or mutualistic symbiosis. These ants raise "herds" of aphids, collecting the sugary honeydew that aphids secrete like a farmer

The yucca plant and yucca moth are an example of mutualistic symbiosis. This kind of relationship suggests origin by direct creation.

might collect milk from a cow. The aphids benefit from the relationship, because the ants are constantly bringing leaf pieces into their chambers and growing fungus to feed the aphids!

Other examples of mutualism abound. The *lichen*, which is the pioneer plant in bare rock succession, is actually a composite plant, consisting of separate species of alga and fungus. The mutualistic relationship is so close that lichens are given their own scientific names and actually propagate themselves in distinct units, even though they are composed of separately identifiable species of fungi and algae.

Our own intestines host a variety of *mutualistic bacteria*, including those that produce vitamin K, which we absorb from our intestine and need for the blood clotting process. In fact, newborn children who have not had a chance to "eat a little dirt" often show a reduced blood-clotting ability until about the eighth day after birth (which is, perhaps more than coincidentally, the time of Jewish circumcision). The bacteria, of course, receive warm, comfortable surroundings and a continuous food supply.

Some of the mutualistic relationships described above are **obligatory**, that is, they are essential to the survival of the two symbiotic species involved. Others, like the association of tickbird and rhinoceros, are **facultative**, which means that they are much looser associations, and species can survive separately, even though they do derive benefit from the relationship.

Many, but not all, mutualistic relationships seem to represent a created level of organization, and it is likely that mutation-selection, acting after the Fall, would only serve to disrupt such relationships. It may be, in fact, disruption of originally created mutualistic relationships that produced the two other types of symbiotic relationships, *commensalism* and *parasitism*.

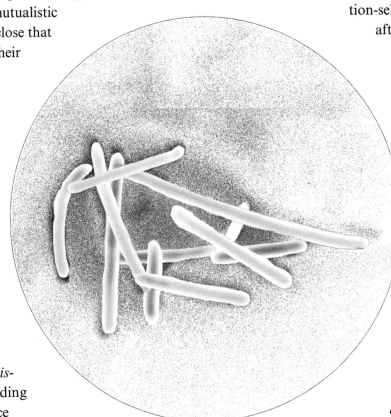

Friendly intestinal bacteria

Commensalism.

Commensalism is a "+0" symbiotic relationship, in which one member of the partnership benefits while the other is unaffected, neither harmed nor helped. Like it or not, the human mouth, digestive cavity, and skin are filled with or covered by a host of commensal bacteria. The bacteria receive the benefit of living in a warm, comfortable environment and receiving abundant nutrients, while we are neither harmed nor helped (except possibly by those villains of so many TV commercials, bad breath and body odor).

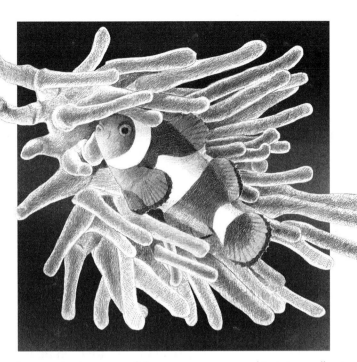

Anemone and anemone fish — sea anemone symbiosis is usually considered commensal, benefitting only the anemone fish. But if the fish actually lures prey into the anemone, then the relationship would be mutualistic.

The shark and remora, a small fish, are commonly cited as a commensal pair. By means of a suction organ on its head, the remora attaches to the shark and is carried along without really interfering with the shark's swimming motion. The remora feeds on the debris left from the shark's preying on some other creature (sharks are sloppy feeders, leaving lots of "table scraps").

Certain small fish can move among the tentacles of sea anemones without discharging their stinging cells. The fish benefits because it can hide from predators among the stinging tentacles, but the anemone gets nothing in return although fish have been observed bringing food to the anemone, which would make the relationship mutualistic.

Parasitism. **Parasitism** is a "+ -" relationship in which one partner benefits and the other is actually harmed. Parasites include a wide variety of creatures. All viruses, several bacteria, some plants, and over half of all known species of animals are parasites. There are **ectoparasites** that attach to the surface of their hosts, such as fleas on a dog; and there are **endoparasites** that live inside the bodies of their hosts, such as tapeworms in the human intestine. Parasites may be nonspecific in the selection of a host, as fleas are, or they may be much more specific, even restricted to certain species or subspecies, qualifying the relationship as symbiotic.

Some parasitic life cycles are quite complex, like that of the Chinese liver fluke (illustrated on following page). The adult lives in the liver. The eggs it lays pass down the bile ducts, into the intestines, and out with the feces. In some areas of the world, human waste ("night soil") is used as fertilizer in rice paddies. The eggs hatch into larvae that bore into snails and multiply there. A second larval stage bores out of the snail and into certain fish living in the marshy rice fields. People sometimes eat these fish raw or undercooked. The parasite is released from the meat, crawls back up the bile ducts from the intestines and re-infects the liver!

Evolutionists have never explained the simple independent steps by which such a complex interdependent cycle could evolve, but Christians don't think God created harmful, parasitic relationships either. Could liver flukes have been created to help us? A lot of valuable iron is dumped into the bile ducts and wasted when the liver filters out old red blood cells. Perhaps these flukes were originally designed to put iron back into the blood stream in return for a little food we weren't going to use anyway. That would benefit both people and the flukes — mutualistic symbiosis!

But then "evolution" spoiled things. Chance mutations may have knocked out mechanisms designed to limit flukes to only a few per liver, and the struggle for survival gave

Metacercariae in flesh
of freshwater fish are
ingested by human host

Free swimming
cercariae

Eggs are
ingested by snail

Embryonic eggs are
passed in fecies

The complex parasitic life cycle of the Chinese liver fluke, Clonorchis (Opisthorchis) sinensis. Such relationships have puzzled creationists as well as evolutionists.

Certain cases of obligate mutualism seem to point clearly to God's power as *Creator*. In the daily operations of these and other ecological relationships, we see God's continuing, ever-present power as *Sustainer* of all that He has made. Various parasitic relationships, however, seem to point to God as *Judge*, the One who changed the world because of man's sin. In Christ's ministry, we see both the power and the promise of God as *Redeemer*. A study of our world, then, tells us not only about God the Creator and Sustainer, but also about God the Judge and Redeemer of all the things that have been made (Romans 1:18–23).

the short-term advantage to the "greedy" flukes, even though long term, it destroyed a relationship originally meant for both their good and ours. Remember, we have other helpful symbionts in our bodies, like the vitamin K bacteria. Many large grazing animals could not survive without a host of mutualistic microbes in their guts to help them with digestion.

Could parasites be degenerate mutualists, designed for good but corrupted by time, chance, struggle, and death (evolution) after sin ruined God's perfect world? Maybe someday you will be the one to find the answer.

<u>God as Creator, Sustainer, Judge, and Redeemer.</u> Symbiotic relationships are a fascinating study in themselves. Like other aspects of God's creation, they testify clearly of God's eternal power and deity (Rom. 1:18–20). Actually, we see more than one aspect of God's power revealed in symbiotic relationships.

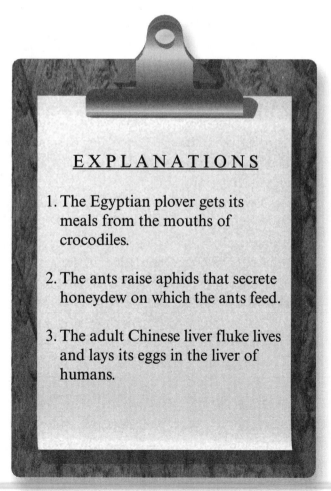

EXPLANATIONS

1. The Egyptian plover gets its meals from the mouths of crocodiles.

2. The ants raise aphids that secrete honeydew on which the ants feed.

3. The adult Chinese liver fluke lives and lays its eggs in the liver of humans.

Questions

Symbiosis

1. Two species living in particularly close interdependence form a relationship called
_____.

2. Name and define the three kinds of symbiosis.

3. Mark the following as examples of mutualism (M), commensalism (C), or parasitism (P):
   a. ____ big predator fish having their teeth cleaned by little fish and shrimp
   b. ____ a plover (bird) pecking gunk out of a crocodile's mouth
   c. ____ bacteria living in the human mouth and skin pores
   d. ____ tag-along remora feeding on scraps from a shark's meal
   e. ____ liver fluke in human bile ducts
   f. ____ yucca moth placing pollen and a few eggs in seed chamber of yucca plant
   g. ____ farmer ants growing fungus gardens for aphids and harvesting their "milk"
   h. ____ lichens, algae-fungi combinations that can grow on bare rock
   i. ____ bacteria in our intestines that produce vitamin K to assist in blood clotting.
   j. ____ the nitrogen-fixing bacteria, *Rhizobium*, in nodules on the roots of legumes
      (beans, peas, alfalfa)
   k. ____ clownfish hiding among the stinging tentacles of a sea anemone

4. Which type of symbiosis may have started when mutations ("evolution") messed up a
complex relationship originally designed for benefit?

5. God's power can be seen in creation (Rom. 1:18–20) in four different ways: Creator,
Sustainer, Judge, Redeemer. Associate each description below with one of these four
aspects of God's power.
   a. _____ completed supernatural acts in the past by which God established the
   perfectly functioning heavens and earth in six days.
   b. _____ continuing "natural" (regular, repeatable) acts in the present by which
   God daily, faithfully upholds His handiwork.
   c. _____ defects, disease, death, and disaster that followed the corruption of the
   world by human sin and the catastrophe of Noah's flood.
   d. _____ the healing Jesus brought while He was on earth, and the return to
   paradise when He comes again.

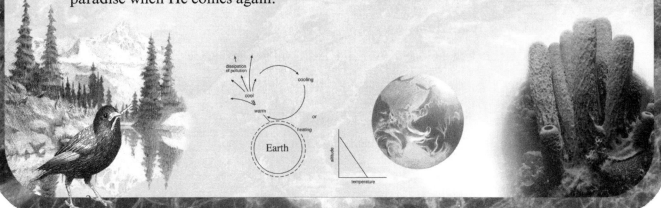

UNIT FIVE:

MANKIND IN THE BIOSPHERE

What is man's proper place in the biosphere? That is one of the most important questions of the 21st century.

Scarcely a hundred years after completing his colonization of most of the New World, modern man has demonstrated his ability to exhaust some of the earth's most valuable and irreplaceable resources, to overload the biosphere with wastes that cannot be recycled fast enough or at all, and, in places, to overcrowd his environment to the detriment of himself and of many other life forms, from endangered species to endangered ecosystems.

Some say man is the problem. They save whales and kill unborn babies. They protect certain field rats and owls, and let farms burn and people go hungry.

The Bible says sin is the problem. The solution is salvation, AND living our faith in Christ. As God's chief stewards, we must "till and keep" (Gen. 2:15) the fabulous garden home God gave us, and "heal and restore" those things that have gone wrong.

Let's take a look now at some of the major problems, including what can and has been done, and what should and should not be done.

Pollution

A **pollutant** is any factor that disrupts normal ecological balance. Pollutants may be harmful or non-degradable substances, such as toxic pesticide residues or non-degradable plastics, or they may be substances not harmful in themselves that are dumped into the ecosystem at a rate too high for proper recycling, such as nitrates and phosphates in detergents and fertilizers.

Lead. Let's start with a success story. Lead was once used in white paint, gasoline (petrol), and plumbing solder. When lead gets into the body, it can't get out. So its effects "magnify" up the food chain to us (as described earlier for mercury and DDT). It builds up until it clogs the "machinery" in living cells (especially protein enzymes), which can lead to brain damage. Some even blame the decline and fall of the Roman Empire partly on excess lead in the plumbing! More down to earth, babies love to chew on things, and lead-based white paint tastes sweet to them. Everyone, of course, had to breathe the lead released into the air from car exhaust.

Fortunately, satisfactory and inexpensive lead substitutes were found for white paint, gas, and solder. The lead problem has been largely solved (except for old homes with old paint and old plumbing).

Cigarette smoke. One of the deadliest forms of air pollution is cigarette smoke, which affects not only the

MYSTERIES OF LIFE

1. Many fish turned up dead in a recreational lake in Iowa.

2. Laundry detergents were smuggled across state lines.

3. A shopping bag was developed that could be boiled and eaten.

*Can You Provide
the Explanations?*

smoker but also the non-smoker who breathes second-hand smoke. In a more personal way, smoking focuses the broader issues of private rights versus public concern. Smokers can claim they have the private right to smoke, but it would seem that that right ends where another person's nose begins. In other words, the claim to private or personal rights can be maintained only if smoking, or any other form of pollution, is kept private and personal. Restrictions on smoking are at least a partial success story, but they also show how emotions can "cloud" an ecological issue.

Nitrates and phosphates. Nitrates and phosphates are fabulous fertilizers that really stimulate plant growth. That sounds great, but unfortunately they illustrate how a pollutant can be "too much of a good thing."

A recreational lake called Sandy Hollow near Sioux Center, Iowa, is a good example. Just after a farmer had fertilized a nearby field one spring, heavy rains washed the nitrates into the lake. The climate turned warm and sunny, and the excess fertilizer stimulated massive growth of algae in the lake — and a massive fish kill followed as the overabundant plants used up far more oxygen than they produced. It took months for Sandy Hollow to recover. Some farms have not recovered from nitrates accumulating below ground where they have poisoned the well water supply (nitrates can cause cancer), forcing some farmers to buy water from town.

Algal blooms/fish kills are common in parts of Florida. The state has mandated retention ponds to catch run-off before it puts fertilizers into rivers, lakes, and bays too much too fast. But now they must make sure the temporary ponds don't become breeding grounds for disease-carrying mosquitoes!

Laundry detergents were adding so many phosphates to the nation's water supply that new formulas had to be developed. Not everyone was pleased with the cleaning, however, and there was some "detergent smuggling" across the country where state laws varied.

Recycling. To be properly recycled through the ecosystem, a substance must not be added too fast and it must be biodegradable — capable of being broken down by microbes or, more loosely, some environmental factor. Things that don't degrade just keep building up in the ecosystem, like many plastics, pesticides, and herbicides once did. Scientists have done a great job of producing most of these things in degradable form — even a shopping bag that can be boiled and eaten (although that never really caught on!)

Recycling bottles and aluminum cans has provided youth with spending money for a long time. But some governments now require recycling. Some citizens have to sort recyclables into three big plastic bins that the local disposal

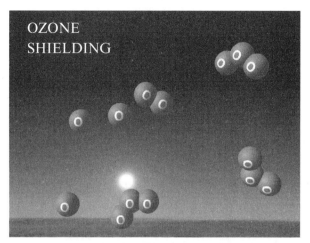

Ozone is formed when high energy ultraviolet radiation from the sun breaks apart molecular oxygen. An oxygen atom then combines with an oxygen molecule producing a new molecule with three atoms of oxygen, ozone.

Ozone is a strong absorber of lower energy ultraviolet radiation which can kill living organisms. This radiation is absorbed by the ozone layer when it breaks the ozone bonds. An oxygen atom is released, but it quickly recombines with another oxygen molecule to regenerate ozone.

company provides. The company sends a truck to pick up all of the recyclables. One begins to wonder about the ecological cost of making all that plastic (which is made from oil or petroleum), of burning all that truck fuel so inefficiently, and of the energy to run the factories to process all those recycled items back into reusable form.

Recycling is definitely a great thing to do, but the ecological benefits have to be weighed against the ecological costs. Paper plates or dishes that must be washed? Washing plates (especially to the health standards needed for restaurants) uses a lot of energy to make the washing water hot, and it puts a lot of detergent waste in our water supply. Paper plates not coated in plastic are biodegradable, and the trees that are used to make paper can be replaced. So . . . which choice is best? What other factors are involved? (Finding or debating the answer might make an interesting project — or try cloth diapers versus disposable!)

It's certainly a good idea to recycle paper, but is it as important as recycling aluminum? Once aluminum is taken out of the ground, it's gone. But after one tree is turned into paper, another can grow to take its place, unless paper

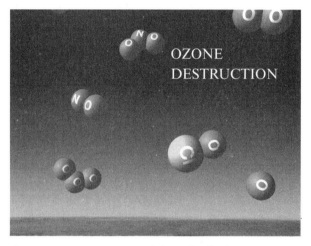

Ozone is very reactive. It easily loses the third oxygen atom in the presence of other highly reactive compounds called radicals, which contain chlorine, hydrogen, nitrogen, or bromine. Minute quantities of these radicals can cause large decreases in ozone because they are not consumed in the reaction. This is called a catalytic cycle.

is being produced and used faster than pulp trees grow. Paper is a **renewable** resource, one that will "grow back" using only the "free" sunlight energy constantly showered on the earth.

Calculating the "cost/benefit" ratio is different for renewable and non-renewable resources, and that's not just the economic cost but the ecological cost as well. After all,

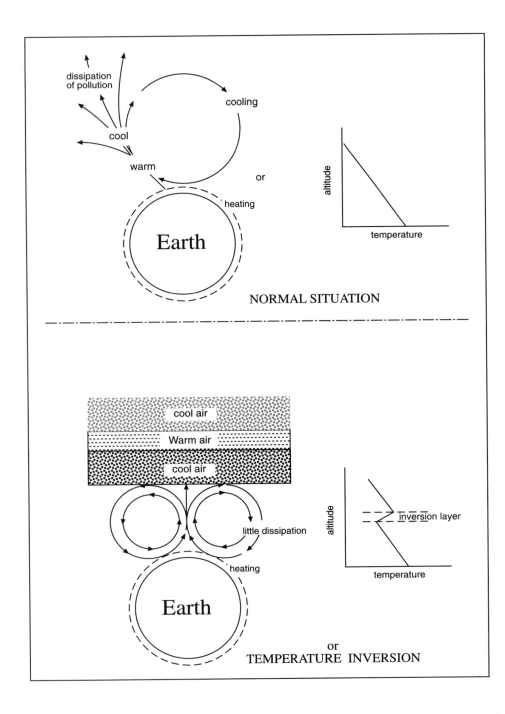

nice — sunshine. The high temperature and pressure inside a car's engine combine oxygen and nitrogen from the air, producing nitrogen oxides like NO_2, nitrogen dioxide. NO_2 forms the yucky brown layer that looks like a dirty blanket covering all but the tallest buildings that can be seen driving down from the mountains into the city (but it also helps produce some spectacularly "eerie" greenish sunsets!).

Ultraviolet (UV) radiation in sunshine acts on NO_2 and O_2 in the air to form a highly corrosive form of oxygen called **ozone** (O_3). Besides being harmful itself, ozone acts on nitrogen oxide and unburned hydrocarbons in auto exhaust to form another corrosive substance, PAN (peroxyacyl nitrate). Thanks to ozone and PAN, Los Angeles air can have an acid-tasting, eye-burning, lung-eating bite to it on smog alert days — and young, old, and ill are wisely advised to stay inside and keep activity to a minimum.

To make matters worse, Los Angeles is beautifully situated in a flat basin between a cool ocean to the south and west and a ring of

collecting old paper and turning it into new uses energy and produces waste products, just like producing new paper from wood.

As can be seen, it will take people with good minds and honest hearts to take care of our planet properly.

Smog. Los Angeles has an abundance of both conditions needed to form photochemical **smog**: (1) lots of automobile exhaust, and (2) lots of something that's otherwise considered quite

very high mountains to the north and east. That's great for postcards, but it's also great for smog-trapping temperature inversions. On the clear, dry nights of semi-arid southern California, land can cool far below the ocean temperature. As the onshore breezes begin in the morning, the warmer air from over the ocean rides up over the cooler, heavier city air, which is trapped against the mountains. Even as the sun warms the land and the city air, it has no tendency to rise into the even warmer air above it. That's called a **temperature inversion**. Air is usually warmed by touching ground warmed by the sun, and that warm air rises into cooler air above, circulating the atmosphere. Temperature inversions trap stagnant air and can allow smog to build up for days.

Not surprisingly, California now has strict standards for car emissions and even vapor recovery hoses at gas pumps. Thankfully, the smog is not nearly as bad as it once was.

Ozone hole — or ozone hoax? Near the ground as part of smog, ozone is a nasty lung-dissolver. But high in the stratosphere, ozone absorbs ultraviolet and thus helps to protect us from skin cancer. (Notice: whether something is a pollutant or not may depend on where it is and how much there is of it.)

Several years ago, scientists noticed some parts of the stratosphere had less ozone than others, with the least amount called an "ozone hole." It was also known that CFCs (**c**hloro**fl**uoro**c**arbons) could start a chain reaction so that a little CFC could destroy a lot of ozone. If that happened high above the earth, it could mean less UV protection and more skin cancer for people down below.

CFCs like freon were used in refrigerators, air conditioners, and in spray cans. Somehow it was decided that the "ozone hole" was caused by people using too many refrigerators and air conditioners and too lazy to pump their own hair spray. Problem: the so-called "ozone hole" is over Antarctica. The O_3 level there varies anyway, and there's no evidence penguins use too much coolant or hair spray. Jet airplane exhaust is sometimes blamed for ozone loss, but again, the least ozone is far from the most jet traffic.

No one who lived through the gas price surge of the 1970s will ever fully trust ecological "doomsday" predictions again. Leading science experts and news reporters everywhere were telling us the earth was about to run out of oil, and cars and civilization would cease to run unless we did something drastic. Gas in some of the larger cities in the United States was rationed and sold to long lines of customers who could only receive gas on alternate days. Then

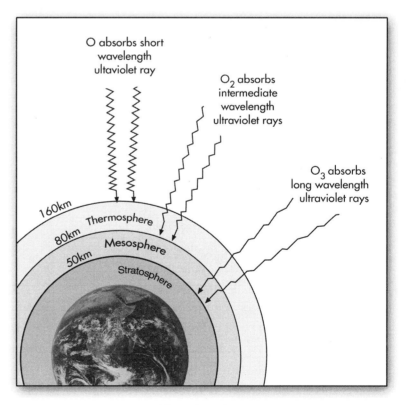

Ultraviolet radiation

suddenly, when the price of gas was right, a world surplus ("glut") of oil appeared!

Unfortunately, it is often very difficult to separate "eco-fact" from "eco-fiction." Environmentalists and politicians who exaggerate eco-problems do us all great harm, both by making themselves hard to believe and by taking time, money, and resources away from real problems that do need attention.

Other pollutants. Not all pollutants are substances. **Noise pollution** is particularly obvious downtown, around airports, or at a rock concert. Aquatic environments can be changed by the addition of warm industrial wastewater — but in some cases a thriving new community of greater biomass and diversity develops at the site of this **thermal pollution**. **Insect pollution** can sometimes be controlled biologically. Green beans protect potatoes from the Colorado potato beetle, for example, and the potatoes protect the beans from the Mexican bean beetle. Planting certain flowers and vegetables together is a beautiful solution to chemical residue problems (and there are books that give the details).

The pollution solution. The scientific solution to the pollution problem is rather obvious. Don't waste resources. Don't add factors to the environment that are harmful or at a rate too fast for the ecosystem to handle. Make things biodegradable. Recycle. Several steps have been taken in this direction. "Conservation" has become a household word; hopefully it has also become a household practice.

Actually, the pollution problems are relatively easy to solve in technological terms. The real problems are social, economic, and religious or philosophical. Most people are in favor of ecological goals, but they waver when they consider the increased costs and decreased convenience to themselves. Failure to live in an ecologically sound manner will result, of course, in unbearably high cost and greatly decreased convenience in the long run. But there's the

catch. In the short run, it is still economically more profitable and personally more convenient to ignore ecology. The same kind of choice faces us that has faced so many other species: short-term versus long-term advantage. Those species that had short-term selective advantage seem to be the ones that in the long run became extinct.

But do we really care about the future? In Scripture, we read the lament of a man who was angry that God did not punish the wicked immediately, because, he said, the wicked are content to enjoy a good life for themselves, without thought for their children. As we shall see throughout, the real solution to our ecological problem must grow out of a religious heart commitment. The basic problem is the "old life" of sin and selfishness (greed); the solution is new life in Jesus Christ!

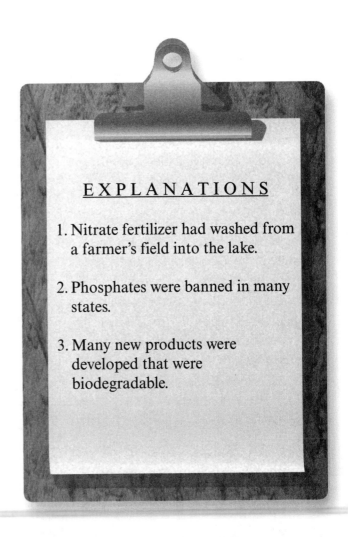

EXPLANATIONS

1. Nitrate fertilizer had washed from a farmer's field into the lake.

2. Phosphates were banned in many states.

3. Many new products were developed that were biodegradable.

1. Anything that disrupts normal ecological balance can be called a _____.

2. What pollutant, once common in white paint, gasoline, and plumbing, has been successfully cleaned up?

3. What problem is there for people who claim the individual right to smoke cigarettes?

4. Nitrates and phosphates are very important and helpful plant nutrients. How can they be pollutants?

5. Recycling of what metal is mankind's best [ecological] success?

6. Which of these resources is renewable: paper, oil, iron, aluminum, plastic?

7. What two ingredients, both common in Los Angeles, are necessary for photochemical smog?

8. Smog problems are worsened where a layer of cool air gets trapped near the ground and warm air "rides" over it, a condition called a temperature _____.

9. Is ozone helpful or harmful? Explain.

10. Is the "ozone hole" a hoax, an exaggeration, a problem, or a problem solved? Defend your answer.

11. What kind of pollution is found both on airport runways and at rock concerts?

12. According to many overzealous environmentalists, the cause of pollution is _____. According to the Bible, the more basic cause of pollution is _____ and the solution is _____.

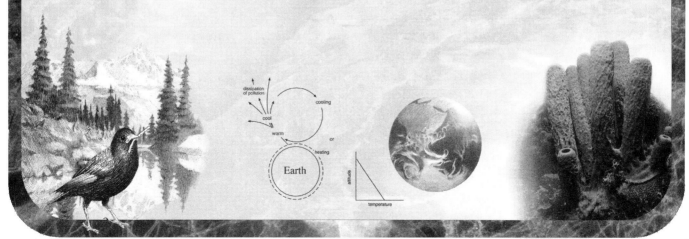

Energy Problems

For perhaps 58 of mankind's 60 centuries (more or less) on the earth, people have used their own muscle power and animal power, and people and animals got their energy from food . . . which is made by green plants . . . which are powered by the sun, which showers us with enough energy to keep the whole biosphere going for a very long time. But then came the internal combustion engine — motors powered by "fossil fuels" — and everything changed!

Fossil fuels. Coal, oil, and natural gas are called **fossil fuels** because they are the remains and products of once-living things buried in rock layers laid down by water in places all over the earth. They are considered a nonrenewable energy source (unlike green plants), since those vast underground deposits are not forming anywhere on the earth today.

Indeed, it seems that fossil fuels were produced, like most other fossils, during Noah's flood. **Coal** is essentially the compressed and charred remains of plants whose stems, leaves, roots, wood, spores, etc. are often remarkably well preserved.

MYSTERIES OF LIFE

1. Rain in Wheeling, West Virginia, once ate through umbrellas and burned people's skin.

2. The *Hindenburg* suddenly exploded while trying to land in New Jersey.

3. Adolf Hitler powered his war machinery on alcohol fuels.

   Can You Provide the Explanations?

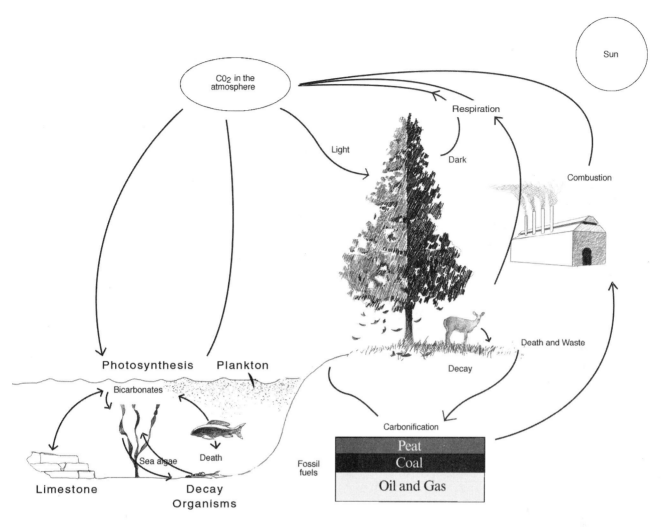

Photosynthesis, respiration, and undersea limestone deposits are all involved in the biogeochemical cycling of the three most abundant elements in living systems, C, H, and O.

Coal has hardly anything in common with swamp or peat bogs, but coal has a lot in common with the deposits in Spirit Lake produced when the volcanic eruption of Mount St. Helens ripped apart a huge forest. The worldwide catastrophe of Noah's time would have produced the similar, but broader, deeper, and more altered deposits we call coal.

Oil is a form of stored energy, like fat, found in the cells of people, plants, animals, and microbes. Oil deposits can't form slowly and gradually from living things dying near the surface, since scavengers quickly gobble up the carcass (including the oil). But if "zillions" of plants, animals, and microbes (and some people?) were buried quickly under a heavy load of sediment — the conditions during Noah's flood — then the oil would be squeezed out and buoyed up through water-laid sand and lime. Some would become trapped under a dome of shale or clay waiting to be discovered as "black gold" or "Texas tea." Underground heating would produce the natural gas deposits often found above the oil.

Natural gas (methane) can also be produced from the decomposition of garbage or compost; oil is secreted by some bacteria; and coal can be made in the lab — but these processes are all too small scale to replace fossil fuels at the rates we are using them. So, fossil

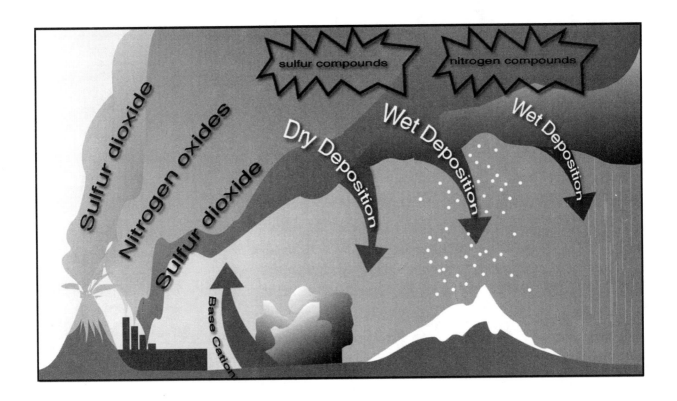

fuels are essentially non-renewable resources. We will eventually run out of them, and they should be used with care.

Still, the fuel reserves are vast, especially of coal, which can be turned into the other two. The bigger problems with burning fossil fuels may be the by-products.

Acid rain. Sulfur (S) is a common impurity in many coal and oil deposits. It's an important chemical extracted for many uses. But sulfur left over and burned with the fuel becomes sulfur dioxide. As raindrops absorb the sulfur dioxide, the reaction with water produces powerful **sulfuric acid**, which then falls as **acid rain**. Raindrops absorbing nitrogen dioxide from smog produce another powerful acid, **nitric acid**, and another form of acid rain.

In the bad old days before pollution controls and smokestack "scrubbers," the coal-mining town of Wheeling, West Virginia, experienced an acid rain strong enough to eat holes in umbrellas and burn the skin. Some say acid rain is dissolving the detail off marble statues, turning Germany's Black Forest into the "Yellow Forest,"

and reducing fish populations in affected lakes. It's expensive, but the problems can, and, in some cases, have been solved.

CO_2 and global warming. Burning fossil fuels produces lots of carbon dioxide, which was once thought to be harmless or even beneficial. After all, green plants absorb CO_2 and turn it into good food.

But some say we are producing too much CO_2 too fast and that the excess will warm the earth, melt the ice caps, flood the coastal cities, change the climate, and bring on drought, floods, and famines. Although one should carefully weigh the (real) evidence as it comes in, this may be an extreme case of eco-exaggeration.

As discussed earlier, CO_2 is a "greenhouse gas," and it does help hold in heat. In fact, the earth seems designed for much more CO_2 and that probably contributed to the milder climate and greater plant growth before the Flood. Global warming would actually be very beneficial biologically — but would the cost be social and economic disaster?

Actually, the earth seems well protected against runaway global warming. The burning of fossil fuels that generates CO_2 that warms the earth also generates dust that cools the earth. A little warming would produce more clouds blocking the sun, thus producing a little cooling. Plants really can make a lot more food from any extra CO_2, and 80 percent of that food is made by plants and microbes in the ocean. CO_2 in water is absorbed to form shells and is also deposited as lime. In short, there are many ecological processes that keep CO_2 levels down, even below levels that would otherwise be beneficial.

It was only a few years ago that some environmentalists were predicting another Ice Age! Several times in recent history large volcanic explosions have produced dust clouds circling the earth, blocking sunlight, producing crop failures, and famine affecting whole nations and civilizations. Volcanoes also release tremendous amounts of CO_2 that could be blamed for global warming — but so far no one has suggested funding a United Nations program to build corks for volcanoes! (The methane gas produced when animals and people eat certain foods could also cause global warming, but so far baked beans have not been banned from picnics!)

It seems clear that problems with global warming and fossil fuels have been greatly exaggerated, robbing time, talent, and money from proper ecological concerns. Still, there are problems, and we should definitely be developing and using alternative energy sources. Sometimes, unfortunately, that involves trading one set of problems for others — and benefits have to be weighed against costs, economic and ecologic.

Electricity. At first glance, electricity looks like a terrific energy source. It can be used to run a wide variety of machines and appliances, and experiments continue with electric cars and "hybrid" gas-electric-inertia cars. Electricity can be produced where flowing water runs turbines, either by natural waterfalls (like Niagara) or at hydroelectric dams. Beautiful park and recreation areas can be built around the dam, and plants and animals usually benefit from the water kept longer in their area.

But most electric power is NOT produced from flowing water; it's produced from burning fossil fuels — so it's back again to the problems with coal, oil, and gas. There are many power plants along the mighty Ohio River, for example, but the river flow is not used to run the energy turbines; it's used instead to float the barges that carry coal. Pollution around such power plants used to be intense, but "scrubbers" and enforcement of clean air standards have helped a lot (though adding to the expense, of course).

It also takes a lot of wire to transmit electricity. Copper wire is getting scarce and expensive, and processing it can produce dangerous pollutants. It takes a lot of maintenance crews (using trucks powered by fossil fuels) to service the lines, and a lot of trees for poles to hold up the wires. Some say the electric and magnetic fields produced around big towers and

109

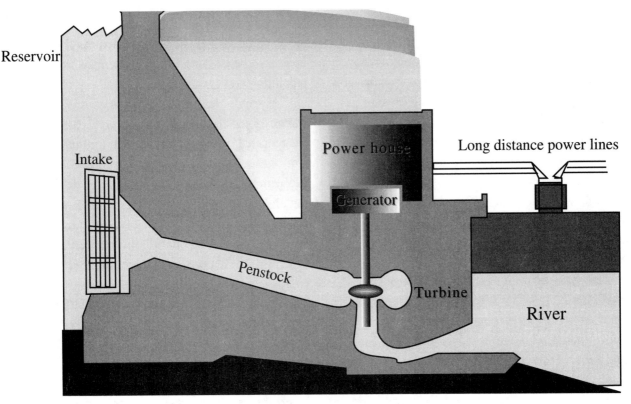

Hydroelectric power plant

transformers can produce health problems, even cancer, in animals and people.

More bad news: electricity is hard to store. It is stored in batteries, but batteries to store lots of electricity are big, bulky, expensive, and full of dangerous chemicals. A real breakthrough in electrical energy storage would be a terrific benefit for all mankind.

Solar power. The sun showers the earth with tremendous amounts of clean, "free" energy. Solar panels, like those seen on space-craft, can convert solar energy into electricity. Problem: it takes a *lot* of solar panels to make a *little* electricity, and even that's only when there's a lot of sun and few clouds. Then there are still the problems of storing and transmitting the electrical energy.

Local energy sources. Solar power makes a lot more sense, of course, in Arizona than in Alaska, and it can be used directly for heating in addition to making electricity. People in Iceland, interestingly enough, have **geothermal** heating

available, heat from hot rocks and geysers within the earth. Actually, the earth a few feet down anywhere is normally warmer in winter and cooler in summer than ground at the surface. This fact can be used to make heat pumps more efficient in cooling and heating. Cleverly, the *body heat* of spectators is used to warm some sports arenas.

The nearly ceaseless strong *winds* blowing over the prairies and through mountain passes can be used to make electricity, if one doesn't mind looking at fields filled with windmills (including some of space age design). The ebb and flow of tides can also be used to make electricity, but the output is not great in most cases. The burning of methane gas produced in the decomposition of garbage and sewage can produce enough electricity to run, or help run, some farms and businesses. Even if none of the local energy sources is entirely sufficient, it saves money, reduces the burden on fossil fuels, and otherwise helps us be good stewards of our resources.

Nuclear energy. A *little* radioactive decay can produce a *lot* of heat, which, in turn, can be used to make electricity. But, besides the storage and transmission of electrical power, there are two other big problems with nuclear energy: safety and waste.

There are many, many safeguards built into a nuclear power plant by knowledgeable scientists and engineers. Still, the near-accidents at Three-Mile Island in Pennsylvania and Chernobyl in the former Soviet Union make people fearful.

Then, radioactive substances are still dangerous even after they are too weak to use as fuels, and they remain dangerous for a very long time. How should we store such wastes, and where?

Some people simply react in fear to the words "nuclear energy." Yet a little nuclear energy can power a submarine full of people safely for months at a time. If safety and waste-disposal problems could really be solved, the result could be a tremendous blessing, especially for people far from other energy sources, or where other sources pollute. The only waste product is warm water used to cool the reactor (as long as no radioactivity escapes).

Portable fuels. Most alternate energy sources are used to make electricity. But it would also be nice to have a fuel that could be carried around without wires, like a can or tank of gasoline or a cylinder of propane.

Hydrogen should be a great fuel. Burning it releases lots of energy, and the only waste is water vapor! Problem: it's *extremely* explosive, and can be set off by static electricity (like the spark made by scuffing shoes across a rug on a cold, dry winter day). Still, some say, putting an odorant in it to signal leaks and taking proper precautions should make it no more dangerous than propane. (But others keep thinking of the *Hindenburg*, a big German dirigible [blimp] filled with hydrogen that exploded and quickly burned while trying to land in New Jersey in 1937.)

Alcohols could be excellent fuels. They are used to fuel some race cars now, and alcohol is added to gasoline in some areas to make "gasohol."

Wind power

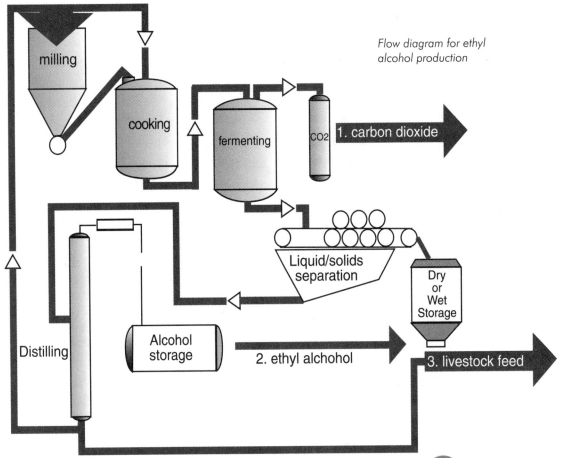

Flow diagram for ethyl alcohol production

milling

cooking

fermenting

CO2

1. carbon dioxide

Liquid/solids separation

Dry or Wet Storage

Distilling

Alcohol storage

2. ethyl alchohol

3. livestock feed

Denied access to petroleum fuels, Hitler powered his World War II war machinery on alcohol fuels. And alcohol, unlike petroleum, is a renewable resource. It is made from fermenting plant materials, and the plants can be grown and harvested year after year.

If scientists can figure out how to remove fermentation inhibitors in wood, alcohol fuels such as butanol could be made from wood chips, yard waste, and garbage! They could also help free us from dependence on those who use their stronghold on petroleum resources as a threat against others.

Many careers in the future are likely to be based on developing and using alternate energy sources. Earth's environment will be helped, and many people will be blessed by those who lead the way.

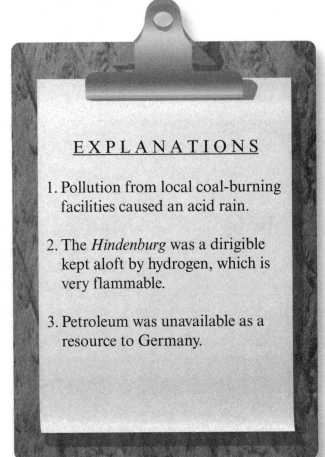

EXPLANATIONS

1. Pollution from local coal-burning facilities caused an acid rain.

2. The *Hindenburg* was a dirigible kept aloft by hydrogen, which is very flammable.

3. Petroleum was unavailable as a resource to Germany.

1. Because they are the buried remains of plants and animals, probably formed worldwide during _____, coal, oil, and gas are called _____ fuels. They can be formed in the lab and in nature, but not as fast as they are used, so they are called _____ (renewable, nonrenewable) resources.

2. Burning sulfur impurities in fossil fuels produces _____ rain, which was harming lakes, forests, and limestone art and structures until the sulfur was removed.

3. Burning fossil fuels produces carbon dioxide, a gas that, like the glass in a _____, helps hold in heat. The earth probably was warmer with greater plant growth before _____, but some fear too much carbon dioxide now would produce "global _____," melting the ice caps and flooding coastal cities. However, many things on the earth would prevent any such overheating, such as _____ and _____ and more carbon dioxide can be produced by one _____ than all mankind's automobiles. Therefore, spending money to lower carbon dioxide production seems like _____ (eco-sense, eco-foolishness).

4. Match the energy sources below with the description of benefits and problems (pros and cons) that follow:

   electricity   **wind**   **nuclear energy**   **solar power**
   body heat   **hydrogen**   **alcohol**   **geothermal heat**

   a. A *little* material produces a *lot* of energy, but the waste products kill living things and last a very long time.

   b. This can be made cheaply from water flowing downhill, but the copper wire delivery system is expensive and non-renewable.

   c. It takes a *lot* of solar panels to collect enough to make a *little* useful energy.

   d. Is very useful in limited areas where hot springs exist and molten rock is near the surface.

   e. A cheap energy source in prairies and mountain passes, but requires fields of propellers.

   f. Is portable and burns clean (producing only H_2O), but highly explosive.

   g. Powers race cars and can be made from fermenting plant wastes, but can be misused and is expensive (until inhibitors to plant breakdown can be removed).

   h. Could possibly be used in large gymnasiums and stadiums.

Preservation and Human Population

Endangered Species. People go all out to preserve the paintings, sculptures, music, and writings of creative human beings. The different kinds of living things are the handiwork of God, so Christians should be leading the effort to preserve these masterpieces of the Master Creator.

But there are crucial differences between God's "created kinds" and some environmentalists' misuse of the word "species." Take the Florida panther, for example. By what was it endangered? Highway traffic? No. Hunters? No. Alligators? No. Habitat reduction? No. It was endangered by evolution, more specifically by mutations.

Mutations are random changes in the hereditary code of DNA. Evolutionists believe mutations are the "raw materials for evolutionary progress." Scientists observe instead that they are a major source of disease, disease organisms, and birth defects (part of the corruption of God's perfect creation). The poor Florida panther had so many

MYSTERIES OF LIFE

1. The Florida panther became an endangered species because of evolution.

2. Not every species should be protected from extinction.

3. Family growth is restricted in some areas of the world.

Can You Provide the Explanations?

mutations affecting it — especially its circulation and reproduction — that no cub born survived one year. The population was down to about 50, and inbreeding in small populations practically guarantees that young will inherit one or more harmful mutations.

The solution has been to cross the Florida panther with panthers from out west. Western panthers have different mutations, and perhaps fewer ones, than the Florida panther. Since most harmful mutations show up in offspring only if both parents carry the same gene, the cross has produced cubs with fewer mutations and a much better chance at survival. But as panthers are on the increase in Florida, the so-called Florida panther is *disappearing* because its genes are mixing with the genes of the other species of western panthers. The Florida panther never was a true species; it was just a sickly **subspecies**, or variety, of a larger created kind.

There's no moral or ecological merit in preserving sickly subspecies as endangered species. Keeping them from breeding with others of their kind only makes matters worse, increasing suffering from mutations. If organisms can interbreed, they belong to the same created kind and should be classified as the same species, not "preserved" in a separate sickly state!

There's an expression: "extinction is forever." That's true for created kinds, but not for subspecies or varieties. Take the quagga, for example, a horse identified by a particular pattern of stripes. It was said to have become extinct early in the 20th century. But now it's being "resurrected" by breeding programs, crossing horses, zebras, and other members of the "horse kind."

Each created kind has a special place in God's web of life and definitely deserves our protection. But let's make sure we are protecting true species, neither sickly subspecies nor varieties that can be bred back again, especially

Florida panther

when we are weighing species protection against human needs.

Some environmentalists say every species (except mankind) deserves equal protection, but are there any ads for "Save the Tapeworm" or "Save the AIDS virus"? People who worship Mother Nature have no way to distinguish between "good and bad" in the environment. A Christian understands that some things are a product of God's creation and deserve protection and preservation; others, such as parasites and disease organisms, reflect the corruption of creation, and can be eliminated. We need the Bible's wisdom more than ever in an age that wants to worship the creature rather than the Creator!

Preserving natural areas. God didn't create living things in isolation, but as parts of complete ecosystems. As reflections of God's creativity, ecosystems also deserve our protection. Some, like rain forests, are filled with so many species that scientists still haven't discovered them all. Others, like Yellowstone, Yosemite,

Zion, Grand Canyon, and Sequoia (Redwoods) National Parks in America are breathtakingly awe-inspiring and lift the hearts of Christians toward God!

Where do people fit in? One extreme says man is an intruder and doesn't belong at all in wilderness areas (or even, some would say, on planet Earth!). The other extreme says man-

kind is all that matters, and people can do whatever they want with their environment. Again, the Bible provides the answer. Ecosystems were created by God with special properties that need to be preserved, understood, and appreciated. But God provided earth as the "garden home" for human beings and told us to take care of it. In fact, if we acted biblically, the earth would be *better* for our presence, not worse.

Recognizing that (in a corrupted creation) Mother Nature can act like a "wicked witch," a Christian ecologist can protect a reef against the ravages of the crown-of-thorns starfish; use controlled burns, but put out extreme fires; try

to stop Dutch elm disease and virus plagues; re-plant mangroves killed in an unusual frost along the south Florida coast; etc. In short, as God's chief stewards, we should try to maintain those things that reflect God's plan for creation ("till and keep") and reduce or eliminate ("heal and restore") the effects of corruption.

Some non-Christians (and even a few Christians, unfortunately) say that God's mandate to "subdue the earth and have dominion" (Gen. 1:28) is a license to exploit. But Jesus said that with Christians it should not be as it is in the world, where leaders get their own way and "lord it over" their subjects. With Christians, Jesus said leaders will give themselves sacrificially to take care of those things (and people) under their authority (Matt. 20:25–28). As "head of the house," for example, a husband is to love his wife, giving himself for her as Christ died for the church — quite a different concept of "leader" than the world has! For a Christian following Jesus' teaching as example, then, "subdue and have dominion" means "to till and keep" and, where things have gone wrong, "to heal and restore."

Population — the People Problem? The Bible says people should benefit the planet, but environment worshipers often say people *are* the problem, the only thing worse than the automobile.

In the late 1960s and '70s, the **population explosion** was billed as the greatest ecological crisis of all. Lots of people produce lots of pollution and use up lots of energy, the propaganda said, and children were pictured as parasites sucking the lifeblood out of the planet.

Is there a population explosion? Suppose we gave each person one square yard (or 1m²) on which to stand, enough room so each could turn around without bumping into anyone else. How much space would all the people in the world take? An area the size of the North American continent? . . . of the 48 contiguous states in America? . . . of the state of Alaska? . . . of San Diego County, California? The answer may be surprising. Even at our present high population of about 6 billion people, all of us, with room to stand without touching each other, would fit into just San Diego County, California! For every person on earth, there are 100 *tons* of termites! Looked at in these ways, mankind is practically an endangered species!

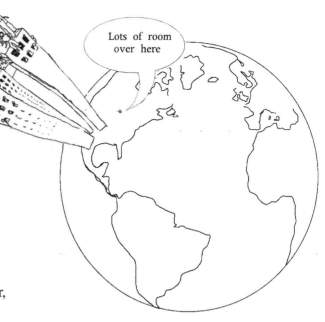

Concentrated areas of population

Living on a ranch in Wyoming or a cattle station in the beautiful outback of Australia, one would wonder what people meant by population explosion. But living in an inner city along America's east coast or in the heart of Tokyo, one would know only too well! So, it's not so much that there are too many people on earth; rather, it's too many people in some areas with room for many more in others. Now that people are no longer dependent on living near farmlands and waterways as we once were, these open areas offer pleasant and often spectacularly beautiful home sites with technology-linked job opportunities.

In the Garden of Eden and again on Ararat after the Flood, God told people to scatter out. But now as then, we disobey and crowd ourselves together in small areas to our own hurt and harm to our garden home.

Unfortunately, however, the total number of people on earth is not the only concern. People, especially in "modern society," make much, much higher demands on the ecology than any animal species. Some people drive in

plastic, plastic, and more plastic — mountains of plastics and bottles and cans burying us and our home!

Is there evidence that all this emphasis on convenience and the fast-paced life has improved the quality of life? Exactly the opposite. There is abundant evidence that the modern emphasis on conspicuous consumption is bad for both our personal health and the health of our garden home. Walking or biking instead of riding in a car; planning one trip to accomplish several goals; choosing products with a concern for others and our garden home, not just a rushed concern for our own convenience; sweating a little in the summer and wearing a sweater in the winter; taking time to "smell the roses" and letting someone else "keep up with the Joneses"; enjoying family and friends and fellowshiping with God are things we can all do for our own health and the health of the fabulous home God has provided for us. In short, live as grateful caretakers (stewards) of all God has put in our care, and enjoy His abundance and fellowship.

air conditioned cars to air conditioned schools and air conditioned offices and stop by several air conditioned convenience stores on the way back to their air conditioned homes — and some complain loudly if the temperature control allows a bead of sweat to form or requires a sweater for comfort! Some cars even offer separate temperature controls for the driver and passenger! Some people even drive rather than walk to a nearby recreation center to get exercise!

Then there is all that wrapping and packaging: disposable plates, disposable diapers, disposable cameras, disposable clothes, even disposable cars, and all those bottles, cans, and

Suppose modern man continues his mad dash for personal convenience and high living. Because each person, especially in a developed country, uses so much energy and produces so much waste, some have argued that the number of children a couple has is *not* a private matter. Right now, China enforces, with severe penalties, a limit of one child per couple. Right or wrong, it does

seem that large populations worsen problems of poverty, pollution, and energy.

It's true that the world population grew at a phenomenal rate through most of the 20th century, and that was in spite of two world wars and devastating famines, plagues, and mass murders under Hitler and Stalin. No longer does anyone doubt that the eight people on Noah's ark could fill the world with people in a few centuries, and certainly in 5,000 years!

Although it receives far less publicity, however, it is also true that many developed countries, including the United States, have already slowed their birth rates to the point called ZPG (**zero population growth**). In America, ZPG is about 2.1 children per family, just enough to balance the death rate.

How did that happen? Strangely enough, the reason for smaller families now may be the same as the reason for larger families in the past — greed. In the bad old days, children were "free help" around the farm, and it paid to have lots of them. Nowadays, children are expensive, a drain on the family budget. Besides many couples today would rather have a bigger house and better clothes than children, and they even put off having children until

they have had enough fun themselves in their younger years. The really good news is that couples who love and want lots of children can have them without fear any longer of being considered burdens on society. So, even though greed and selfishness are not admirable motives themselves, God can use this worldly attitude to benefit His people.

Many Christians these days also choose to limit their families, not for selfish reasons, but so that they can provide

guide or object of worship, and people apart from God are too full of greed and too empty of wisdom.

"The earth is not our mother; it's the home our Father gave us." "The earth was once a perfect place, a gift of love not war," a product of God's creation, to till and keep. But our garden home experienced the corruption of man's sin and the catastrophe of Noah's flood, and, following the example of Christ, we need to heal and restore those things gone wrong.

How will we treat our home? Will we trash it like disinterested renters just passing through, looking to get the most for ourselves with the least effort? Or will we act as grateful caretakers, thrilled and eager to take care of and repair the fabulous garden home God prepared for us? The world is watching. The Christian concept of stewardship is much better explained by deeds than by words.

more effectively for their growth and training. Although God commanded people to multiply and fill the earth, that does not mean each couple must have the maximum number of children possible. Indeed, the apostle Paul tells us that Christians may rightfully choose to remain single, devoting themselves to God. In faithful prayer, honestly seeking the Lord's will, some couples may conclude God would have them limit family size whereas others believe God has and will provide all they need for a very large family. "Thy will be done." In either case, the Bible tells us children are fantastic, a heritage from the Lord, and happy are the mother and father who have their "quiver full of them," whatever size that quiver might be (Ps. 127:5).

Pollution Solution; Christian Stewardship. It's studying God's Word, seeking His will, and putting our faith into practice that is really the key to solving *all* our ecological problems, tilling and keeping the garden home God gave us, and healing and restoring things that have gone wrong. Mother Nature is too brutal to be our

EXPLANATIONS

1. Their endangerment was caused by mutations.

2. Harmful viruses and detrimental organisms should be allowed to become extinct.

3. There is plenty of room in the world for billions of people.

1. Christians should lead the fight to preserve real endangered species because they are the handiwork of _____. But it's harmful and wasteful to try to preserve sickly subspecies endangered by "evolution" (too many mutations), such as the _____. So far, even people who want to save whale babies more than human babies are not really trying to preserve species like _____.

2. Should Christians try to preserve ecosystems as well as true species (created kinds)? Why or why not?

3. When the Bible tells us (through our first parents) to "subdue the earth and have domin-ion," does that mean we're the boss and can do whatever we want with the earth? Why or why not?

4. If you gave each person on earth a square yard (or square meter) to stand on (so each could turn without touching others), an area the size of _____ (North America; the United States; the state of Alaska; or the county of San Diego) would hold six billion people. Does that sound like a devastating population explosion? Has the balance of births and deaths in the United States and many other "developed" countries reached ZPG (zero population growth)?

5. True or false: There may not be too many people on the earth, but problems can arise from too many living too close together, and from each person in "modern society" using lots of energy and resources.

6. Remember, "the earth is not our mother; it's the _____ our Father gave us." What should be our attitude toward our "garden home"? We should be good _____, following God's command "to till and _____" (Gen. 2:3), and following Christ's example where things have gone wrong in our sin-ruined world, "to heal and _____."

Answers to Chapter Questions

Chapter One

1. delight
2. ecology
3. Mankind's sin ruined God's perfect world and brought struggle and death
4. keep; restore
5. creaton → corruption → catastrophe → Christ (Christ is also the Creator who could be listed first — the Alpha and Omega, the First and Last)
6. a. catastrophe
   b. corruption
   c. creation
   d. Christ
7. evolution
8. Bible

Chapter Two

1. ecosystem
2. community or biotic; environment or abiotic (or physical factors)
3. a. grassland (or forest, desert, lake, etc.)
   b. puddle (or pond, rotting log, etc.)
   c. aquarium or terrarium, etc.
4. "spaceship earth"
5. web
6. yes
7. No, because the plants couldn't survive without the pollinators.
8. plants and animals
9. ecological equivalents
10. kangaroo, zebra, and bison — large grazers in grasslands in different biogeographic realms (or ostrich, emu, rhea; lion, tiger, cougar; etc.)
11. biogeographic
12. Australia (or Australian)
13. no; no; migration from Ararat after Noah's flood seems to be the key (with the "kinder, gentler" marsupials forced to move farthest by the more competitive placental mammals, thus arriving in Australia first and before the land bridge they used "drowned" and prevented placentals from following).

Chapter Three

1. biomes
2. a. desert
   b. taiga
   c. tundra
   d. tundra
   e. desert
   f. desert
   g. grassland
   h. deciduous forest
   i. grassland
   j. deciduous forest
   k. chaparral
   l. tropical rain forest
   m. chaparral
   n. tropical rain forest
   o. taiga
3. biosphere

Chapter Four

1. 39° F or 4° C; because water is heaviest (densest) at that temperature and sinks
2. a. true
   b. true
   c. true
   d. true
   e. true
3. blooms; red tide
4. aphotic zone; dead things and waste products falling from above
5. a. planktonic
   b. nektonic
   c. benthic
6. Many forms can attach to rocks and hold on against tides and waves; sand keeps shifting, and few things (except burrowers) can stay there permanently.
7. reefs

8. a. fringing
   b. barrier
   c. atoll

9. yes; yes — a good example of God's provision for healing and restoration

10. both — God is both the great scientist and great artist.

Chapter Five

1. photoperiod (day length variation)

2. Nome, Alaska

3. to measure the length of night (for plants whose sprouting, fruiting, leaf drop, etc. depend on photoperiod)

4. any of the following: seed sprouting, flowering, fruiting, leaf drop, animal migrations, mating, egg laying, etc.

5. cold

6. hibernation; summer sleep

7. stars, magnetic field, smell, landmarks

8. daily (24 hours); insect activity, human peak activity, opening and closing of morning glory flowers, etc.

9. SAD

Chapter Six

1. carbon dioxide and water vapor

2. the greenhouse effect — more carbon dioxide (before fossils, fossil fuels, and limestone kept carbon dioxide from being recycled after Noah's flood) and perhaps a water vapor canopy around the earth before the flood

3. heterothermal

4. psychrophile (or cryophile), mesophile, thermophile

5. obligate

6. soil

7. leaching; it's possible that it did not rain on the earth until the Flood, with pre-Flood plants nourished by mist and springs that brought minerals up to plant roots.

8. Some release the extra salt through tears; others excrete a very concentrated urine.

9. limiting factor

Chapter Seven

1. pleasant; food

2. photosynthesis

3. water and carbon dioxide (either order); sugar; oxygen

4. six; no; just rearranged

5. conservation; matter

6. respiration

7. water and carbon dioxide (either order); yes; stays the same

8. biogeochemical

9. the atmosphere; nitrogen fixers; soil fertility would fall dramatically and food shortages and famines would follow.

10. biodegradable

11. decomposers (or recyclers)

12. true

13. producers; consumers

14. herb-; carn-; omn-

15. no; yes; flying fox, parrot, grizzly bear; ripping and slashing into fruit or holding and prying open seed; no

16. not in the biblical sense; no; the Bible uses the Hebrew word *nephesh* to describe the "life force" that God gave to animals and people — not plants

Chapter Eight

1. producer, herbivore, carnivore, top carnivore

2. (top) carnivores; magnification

3. producers; top carnivores

4. second law

5. 1,000 tons; carrying

6. 10 lbs. (or kg). The family could have 100 lbs. (or kg) of grain for themselves instead of 10 lbs. of beef.

7. the sun; green plants

8. The sun is shrinking as it burns itself out. In the new heavens and new earth, the energy source will be the Son, Jesus Christ.

Chapter Nine

1. scavengers; predators

2. prey. When prey are scarce, predators

starve or have fewer young, and their population declines.

3.

4. no; After man's sin brought death into the world, some (and only some) animals with sharp teeth and/or claws began using them to kill other animals. When the prey population got too low, the predators declined, allowing the prey to come back, thus allowing the predators to increase, starting the cycle over again — all with God's permission in a fallen world, but not with God's creativity.

5. territoriality

6. birds singing, dog urinating, etc.; ritualistic combat, like "singing duels" between birds; walrus (or seal, albatross, etc.)

7. yes; desert plants that space themselves by secreting inhibitors from their roots

8. no; Both sides in ritualistic combat have to be designed not to kill each other, and evolution can't plan for two different things to happen at the same time in the same place. "Evolution" could destroy territoriality by accidentally knocking out just one gene in the complex instinct, and struggle would reward the killer — until prey control kicked in.

Chapter Ten

1.

2. lemming (or snowshoe hare, etc.); out of control

3. using weed killers (herbicides) and pest or insect killers (insecticides or pesticides), such as DDT and rat poison, are examples

of artificial chemical controls; using a virus to control rabbits, sterilizing male flies, or using "gyplure" male sex attractant to control moths are examples of artificial biological control.

4. a. Chemicals kill other things and build up to poisonous levels in the environment, such as DDT or mercury

   b. the starling from England that eliminated spanworms in Central Park, but then spread out across the country to crowd out native song birds

   c. The examples in the second part of question 3 were all successful.

Chapter Eleven

1. succession

2. pioneer; climax; seral

3. lichens

4. lichens → mosses → ferns → shrubs → trees

5. protozoans → worms → insects → birds → mammals

6. In real succession, plants and animals already living in other places move in as conditions change (migrations); in imagined evolution, accidental changes in heredity are supposed to turn lichens into moss, moss into ferns, etc. (mutations). Real succession happens relatively fast — a few years, decades, or maybe a century for tough environments; imagined evolution supposedly takes millions of years, unobservable to science.

7. steno; index

8. sand dune

9. filling in of ponds and small lakes

10. secondary; fast; like

11. a. BF
    b. AF
    c. AF
    d. BF

e. BF

f. AF

g. BA

Chapter Twelve

1. niche; habitat

2. (Answers may vary.) Some woodpeckers eat insects and save trees from destruction; they drill holes to make nests for themselves that can be used for others; they help break down dead wood; some woodpeckers store acorns that are also eaten by others; they are also "home" for lice, ticks, intestinal parasites, and may provide food for a wild cat; their beauty and design point us to God.

3. micro

4. adaptations

5. evolution; God (or creation); creation

6. (Answers may vary.)

   a. honeybee — pollen comb, pollen basket, antenna cleaner; other — "zippers" in feather barbs; "drilling tools" for woodpeckers; tongue sheath for woodpecker; hinge on hammer orchid

   b. honeybee — making honey and royal jelly; other — bombardier beetle's "cannon"; hormones producing directional growth in plants

   c. honeybee — round and waggle dances; navigation by sun; cool hive; other — instincts and imprinting

   d. honeybee — social castes (queens, drones, workers, etc.); other — ritualistic combat (top dog/under dog, etc.)

Chapter Thirteen

1. symbiosis

2. mutualism — both species benefit; commensalism — one benefits, the other is unaffected; parasitism — one benefits, one is harmed

3. a. m

   b. m

   c. c

   d. c

   e. p

   f. m

   g. m

   h. m

   i. m

   j. m

   k. c (or perhaps m if the fish helps feed the anemone)

4. parasitism

5. a. Creator

   b. Sustainer

   c. Judge

   d. Redeemer

Chapter Fourteen

1. pollutant

2. lead

3. the second-hand smoke is harmful to others

4. They are great fertilizers and can stimulate too much growth of algae (blooms) that can kill fish, and excess nitrates in the water supply can cause cancer.

5. aluminum

6. paper (of those listed, only paper can be replaced as fast as it is used)

7. automobile exhaust and sunshine

8. inversion

9. Ozone is a harmful part of smog near the ground, but up in the stratosphere it absorbs UV rays and helps protect us from cancer.

10. Possibly a problem solved; chemicals in spray pumps and refrigerators can break down ozone in the lab and they have been greatly reduced, but the "ozone hole" may not have been caused by these things in the first place.

11. noise pollution

12. people; sin (greed, selfishness); Jesus Christ (salvation)

Chapter Fifteen

1. Noah's flood; fossil fuels; nonrenewable

2. acid

3. greenhouse; Noah's flood; warming; (possible answers): cooling from the dust produced and extra clouds formed, more food production from photosynthesis; volcano; eco-foolishness

4. a. nuclear energy
   b. electricity
   c. solar power
   d. geothermal heat
   e. wind
   f. hydrogen
   g. alcohol
   h. body heat

Chapter Sixteen

1. God; the Florida panther; tapeworms, smallpox and other viruses. (Note: It's certainly fine to save the panther in Florida by crossing it with healthier panthers, but then it won't be the "sickly" Florida panther anymore.)

2. yes; both because God created whole ecosystems and because each created kind needs its whole ecosystem to do its best

3. no; according to the Bible and Jesus' words and example, the "boss" or "lord" is to be servant of all, nurturing and taking care of those under his/her authority

4. San Diego County; no; yes

5. true

6. home; our attitude should be one of gratefulness and eagerness to care for the home God has provided for us; stewards; keep; restore

Index

Glossary

Note: Italicized words in a definition are found defined elsewhere in the glossary. Page numbers for these and additional words are found in the index.

abiotic — Referring to physical factors in an ecosystem, such as light, temperature, minerals, etc.

adaptation — (1) Design feature (see *adaptations* below); (2) Process by which multiplying species express different features as they move into new environments or meet changes in existing environments because (a) they express the range of variation God built into each kind when he created them to "multiply and fill the earth" or (b) according to evolution, chance mutations change one kind of life into another, which then kills off the competition and takes its place.

adaptations — Design features that suit each kind of life to its particular role in God's overall plan for the earth, including (a) structural adaptations like the pollen basket on a honeybee's leg or "drilling tools" of the woodpecker; (b) functional adaptations such as the powerful spray of the bombardier beetle or inhibitors secreted by the roots of desert plants; (c) behavioral adaptations such as the honeybee's dance or the ritualistic combat of territorial birds; (d) social adaptations such as the caste system (queens, workers, drones) of termites or top dog/underdog pack behavior in wolves.

altitude/latitude relationship — Going up 1,000 feet (300 m) is equivalent in ecological effect to traveling 600 miles (1,000 km) toward either pole.

aphotic — "without light"; often referring to waters deeper than 600 feet (200 m).

Ararat — The mountainous region (in the country of Turkey today) where Noah's ark landed, thus the center for migration in the world after the worldwide Flood (see pages 12–14).

auxins — Plant hormones responsible for many effects, including directed growth movements (*tropisms*) toward or away from light, gravity, water, etc.

bare rock succession — Ecological progression from bare rock to forest as a result of increased soil depth, moisture, and shade produced by a series of plant *communities* (*lichen* to moss to fern to shrub to tree) paving the way for a series of animal communities (protozoan to worm to insect to bird to mammal).

biodegradable — Capable of being broken down and recycled through the ecosystem, especially by bacteria.

biogeochemical cycle — The circular flow (cycle) of matter (-chemical) from the earth (-geo) to living things (bio-) and back again; based on the law of conservation of matter, as seen in the *nitrogen cycle* and the balance between *photosynthesis* and *respiration*.

biogeographic realm — (1) One of the six major continental areas each separated from the others by a major ecological barrier: Palearctic, Nearctic, Neotropical, Ethiopian, Oriental, Australian (see pages 12–13); (2) A major geographic area with different kinds of plants and animals playing similar ecological roles (e.g., bison, zebras, and kangaroos, respectively, as *ecological equivalents* in the grasslands of Nearctic, Ethiopian, and Australian realms); (3) Geographic differences among plants and animals possibly established by migration from the mountains of Ararat following Noah's flood (see pages 12–14).

biological control — The process where scientists use a certain species or some biological agent to control the population of some harmful or disruptive species, such as using a virus to control explosive rabbit populations in Australia, or using "ladybugs" to control destructive aphids; usually ecologically preferable to *chemical control*.

biological magnification — The tendency for poisonous substances (toxins, such as lead and DDT) to increase in amounts up the food chain, so that they have greater harmful effects on *top carnivores* than on *herbivores* or *producers*.

biomass — Amount of living and once-living material in an environment.

biomes — One of the seven* major climate-controlled continental ecosystems: desert, chaparral, grassland, tropical rain forst, deciduous forest, taiga (coniferous forest), or tundra. (*Others may list six, nine, or more.)

biosphere — All living things on the earth and their environments; the global ecosystem.

biotic — Referring to life (e.g., the amount of grass is a biotic factor affecting the number of grazers in an area).

bloom — Explosive growth of algae in a body of water, usually stimulated by sunny, warm conditions and/or influx of nutrients (natural or artificial); the abundant green plants may use up so much oxygen at night that fish die.

carnivore — Meat eater; *predators* and *scavengers* that play important roles in the earth's ecosystem after mankind's *sin* and before *Christ's* return.

carrying capacity — The amount of living creatures an area can support (e.g., the number of grazers a prairie or pasture can maintain).

catastrophe — The worldwide flood of Noah's time (about 4,500–5,000 years ago) that dramatically changed the earth's ecology (see pages 81–82).

chaparral — Warm, sunny *biome* with gentle winter rains around the Mediterranean Sea and in Southern California, very pleasant for people — except for the frequent fires.

chemical control — The process where scientists use man-made chemicals to control pest population, such as spraying DDT to control insects or spraying herbicides to kill weeds; usually considered more ecologically disruptive than biological control.

CHONPS — Acronym for the symbols of the five major elements required for plant growth, and animal and human life; Carbon, Hydrogen, Oxygen, Nitrogen, Phosphorus, and Sulfur.

Christ — (1) Jesus, the eternally begotten son of God, the Word who was with God as Creator in the beginning "without whom was not anything made that was made" (John 1:1–4); (2) Jesus, the Redeemer who died for our sins and saved us from death; (3) The One who is coming again to make a "new heavens and earth" with perfect peace and harmony restored as the fourth of the "four Cs" of biblical history (creation, corruption, catastrophe, Christ) (see 2 Peter 3).

circadian rhythms — Cycles that repeat daily, such as the unfolding of leaves and petals in some plants and times of peak activity in some animals and people.

climate — The average annual conditions of precipitation (rain or snow), temperature, and day length in an area, including seasonal variation.

climax — The final stage in ecological *succession*, usually the *community* with the greatest diversity and *biomass* that can continue to reproduce itself in a given environment.

commensalism — ("+0") *Symbiosis* that benefits one species and leaves the other unaffected, such as the remora that "rides along" on a shark and eats "leftovers" from the shark's meal.

community (ecological community) — The plants, animals, microbes, and people in an area, i.e., the living parts of an *ecosystem*.

conservation of matter, law of — (1) Ecological processes do not create new atoms, so matter must be recycled, as illustrated by the balance between photosynthesis and cellular respiration:

photosynthesis

$$6H_2O + 6CO_2 \rightleftarrows C_6H_{12}O_6 + 6O_2$$

respiration

(2) Only God can create or destroy matter/energy, so physical processes cannot change the total amount of matter/energy in the universe.

consumers — All living things (people, animals, *decomposers*, and most microbes) that get their food by eating green plants (*producers*) or something that ate green plants.

corruption — (1) The ruin of God's perfect world by mankind's sin, bringing the beginning of pain, disease, disaster, defects, predation, aging, and death; (2) The tendency of things left to themselves to run down, described in Scripture as the "bondage to decay" (Romans 8) and the "heavens growing old and wearing out" (Hebrews 1); (3) The tendency of systems left to themselves to lose order, useful energy, or information, described in science as the *second law of thermodynamics*.

creation — (1) The completed supernatural acts by which God in Christ brought forth from nothing beyond himself all time, matter, energy, and space during six days of the creation week; (2) The time before mankind's sin when plants, animals, microbes, and people all lived together in perfect harmony without pain, disease, or death; (3) The orderly universe brought into being by God; the object of a scientist's study.

cryophile (psychrophile) "cold living" — Plant, animal, or microbe designed to thrive at low temperatures, such as snow algae or polar bears (which also do very well at moderate temperatures).

deciduous forest — Most productive *biome*, including many animals, centers of civilization, and trees whose leaves change color and drop in the fall.

decay — (1) The helpful process of decomposition and recycling present at creation: (2) The harmful "bondage to decay" or *corruption* (Romans 8), or the universe "growing old and wearing out" (Hebrews 1), that began after mankind's *sin* and will end when *Christ* comes again.

decomposers — Bacteria, fungi, and other creatures that break down materials for recycling.

desert — *Biome* that, hot or cold, receives less than six inches (15 cm) of rain per year, ranging from barren sand and rock to environments with many well-spaced plants and animals designed to thrive there.

ecological equivalents — Different plants and animals playing similar ecological roles in different geographic areas (possibly as a result of migration patterns from Ararat), such as kangaroos, zebras, and bison as major grazers in Australia, Africa, and America, respectively. (See *biogeographic realms*; also see pages 12–14.)

ecologist — a scientist who studies ecology.

ecology — The study of (-ology) our home (eco-, or oikos), i.e., the study of plants, animals, microbes, and their environment in relation to one another and to mankind.

ecosystem — A community of living things (plants, animals, microbes, and people), their *environment*, and the ways each depends on the others; an ecosystem can be large (Great Plains) or small (mud puddle), natural or artificial (aquarium).

edaphic climax — *Ecosystem* whose final form (*climax*) depends more on *soil* factors than on *climate*.

Eden — The perfect "garden of delight" God created as the home for our first parents, Adam and Eve. There was no suffering or death in Eden, but mankind's sin brought struggle, disease, disaster, and death into the world God had created "all very good." (See Genesis chapters 1–3.)

endangered species — A variety of life whose numbers are so low that it must be protected from extinction (a) because it is the handiwork of God with an important, even if unknown, place in the web of life He created, (b) unless it is merely a sickly subspecies (see *Florida panther*) that should be allowed to breed with others of its created kind, or (c) a variety — not a true species — that could be bred from others of its kind (like the quagga), and so is not truly in danger of extinction.

environment — Physical (*abiotic*) factors, such as light, temperature, minerals, etc., surrounding and interacting with living things.

estivation — summer sleep, in contrast to hibernation, a form of energy conservation for some animals living in very hot environments.

estuary — Place where fresh water flows into saltwater; a rich and diverse *habitat* providing a home for the young of many kinds of life.

eury- — Prefix used for creatures that can survive a wide range of some ecological factor, (e.g., euryhaline and eurythermal are used for living things that can handle a wide variety of salt [-haline] and temperature [-thermal] conditions.)

eutrophication — Pond succession; the tendency for ponds and small lakes to fill with aquatic plants and for "meat-eating" game fish to be replaced by vegetarians (a natural process usually opposed by swimmers, boaters, and fisherman).

evolution — The belief (based on what Charles Darwin called "the *war of nature*") that millions of years of struggle and death produced all plants, animals, microbes, people, and all ecological relationships without any necessary help from God, and that struggle and death will continue for million of years until finally death wins. (See also *succession*.)

facultative — Helpful, but not necessary for survival, such as the *mutualistic* relationship between rhinoceros and tickbird. (See also *obligate*.)

Fall — See *corruption*.

fauna — The animals in an area.

fittest — The plant, animal, microbe, or person that leaves the greatest number of offspring to the next generation (which means that "survival of the fittest" is only "survival of the survivors" and does NOT necessarily either improve adaptations or change a species into something else.)

Flood (Noah's flood) — See *catastrophe*.

flora — The plants in an area.

Florida panther — A variety (NOT a true species) of panther endangered by "evolution" (*mutations*) which produced so many defects in its circulation and reproduction that no young could survive to maturity; crossing it with western panthers with different mutations did produce offspring that could survive — but they are no longer a "Florida panther," a sickly subspecies, but a healthier panther instead.

food chain — A list of creatures from *producers* through top *carnivores*, showing "who eats whom."

food pyramid — Diagram showing the relative amount (in energy, mass, or weight, or numbers) of living material at each link or level of a food chain; the amount of food often decreases by 90 percent (10 percent saved) at each step.

food web — Diagram showing what creatures eat what, usually more complex than a food chain because many organisms have several different food sources.

fossil fuels — Coal, oil, and natural gas, which were produced from the remains of plants, animals, microbes, and people fossilized largely during Noah's flood (and, therefore, not renewable on a large scale today). (See also global warming.)

four Cs — A summary of biblical history that helps us to understand ecology: (1) God's perfect world (creation), (2) ruined by mankind's *sin* (*corruption*), (3) destroyed by Noah's flood (*catastrophe*), (4) restored to new life (*Christ*).

global warming — The fear that CO_2 production from burning fossil fuels (coal, oil, gas) will produce a runaway *greenhouse effect*, overheating the earth, melting the ice caps, flooding coastal cities, and destroying farming by changing climate; actually, the earth has many means of "absorbing" CO_2 (see pages 37–38), and present levels are probably far below biologically beneficial pre-Flood CO_2 levels.

grassland — Grassy *biome* with herds of large grazing animals that makes very productive farmlands (the world's "breadbaskets").

greenhouse effect — The tendency of certain gases in the atmosphere, especially CO_2 and H_2O vapor, to hold in heat for the earth like glass traps and holds heat from sunlight in a greenhouse, an effect that probably helped produce a milder pole-to-pole climate before Noah's flood (but some fear it will produce excessive "global warming").

habitat — The place a creature lives, usually described in terms of climate (light, temperature, moisture), soil conditions, and surrounding plants and animals.

"heal and restore" — The suggestion by this book's author that on the basis of Christ's example, God's stewardship command in a corrupted creation might be changed form "till and keep" to "heal and restore."

herbivore — Plant eater; During the creation period before mankind's sin, all living things were herbivores (even those with sharp teeth and claws — see page 48).

heterothermal — Animals whose body temperature may go up and down with the temperature of their surroundings, although they can raise or lower their temperature behaviorally, (e.g., by sunning themselves, seeking or avoiding shade and burrows, limiting activity, holding certain body parts toward or away from the sun, etc.); improperly called "cold-blooded," though most are sluggish at cold temperatures.

homothermal — People and most animals which keep their body temperature constant by internal physiological means that involve, for example, nerve and hormone control of blood flow to/from the surface and appendages, and sweating or panting; improperly called "warm-blooded."

hydrologic cycle (water cycle) — Water evaporating from oceans, lakes, and rivers, returning through condensation, producing rain and snow.

Ice Age — The polar and high-mountain build-up of ice caps and glaciers following Noah's flood that covered 30 percent of the earth's continents within perhaps 500 years and still covers 10 percent of the continents today.

index species — A kind of plant, animal, or microbe that lives only in a certain environment, therefore acting as a marker (index) for that ecosystem.

instinct — Complex behavior pattern programmed ahead by God so that it can be expressed without learning or practice, such as nest building, courtship rituals, and some migratory behavior.

J-shaped population growth — The "boom and bust" population growth of animals like lemmings and snowshoe hares, in which numbers increase sharply then drop catastrophically before building up rapidly again.

Judge — God's role as the One who imposed the righteous and forewarned penalty for mankind's *sin*, bringing defects, disease, death, and disaster (*corruption* and *catastrophe*) into our fallen world; but His role also as the One who will accept Jesus' life, death, and resurrection as payment for our sin, releasing us form pain and death forevermore.

law of conservation of matter — See *conservation of matter.*

leaching — Minerals washing down and out of *soil*, which produces poor soils in areas of heavy rainfall; before Noah's flood, minerals may have been brought up to plant roots through springs, the opposite of leaching.

legumes — Group of plants (including beans, peas, and alfalfa) that enrich soil because of the nitrogen-fixing bacteria (*rhizobium*) that live (in mutualistic symbiosis) in nodules on their roots.

lichens — "Compound" plants composed of green algae that can make food by photosynthesis and fungi that can absorb water and dissolve rock, examples of mutualistic symbiosis serving as *pioneers* in *bare rock succession.*

mammal — Animal kinds that have at least some hair and nourish their young on milk, whether they lay eggs (*monotremes*, like the platypus), have pouches (*marsupials*, like the kangaroo), or nourish their young through an exchange organ in the mother's womb called a placenta, like dogs, cats, cows, etc. have.

marsupials — *Mammals* like kangaroos and koalas that give birth to very tiny young and raise them to maturity in the mother's pouch.

microhabitat — The very specific conditions experienced, for example, by a beetle in a rotting log, a glow-worm in a cave, or a parasite in the human liver (in contrast to the climate and soil conditions of the general habitat).

monotremes — Mammals, like the platypus, that lay eggs.

"Mother Nature" — The belief that (1) the earth, not God, produced all life and ecosystems; (2) the earth is our "mother," not the home our Father gave us, and/or (3) nature is our guide, not God's rules for right and wrong or good and bad (even when Mother Nature acts like a wicked witch; see page 116).

mutations — Random changes in heredity observed by scientists to produce birth defects, disease, disease organisms, and early death, but thought by evolutionists to change one kind of life into other, better-adapted ones.

mutualism — ("++") *Symbiosis* that benefits both species involved, such as the relationship between yucca plant and yucca moth, farmer ants and aphids, humans and vitamin K bacteria, legumes and nitrogen-fixing bacteria, rhinoceros and tickbird, crocodile and plover. (See index for details on preceding examples.)

natural selection — (1) The belief of evolutionists beginning with Darwin that a constant struggle to the death among members of the same species ("survival of the fittest") will gradually change that species into a new and improved kind of life; (2) The observation that each kind of life produces individuals with a wide variety of traits, some surviving more easily in one environment and some in another (which means that generalized ancestors would have tended to break up into specialized subtypes as the created kinds multiplied and filled the earth after the Fall and the Flood.)

nephesh — Hebrew word for the "life force" that people and animals have that plants do not have (meaning that eating plants, which God created for food, is NOT an example of death before mankind's *sin*).

niche — (pronounced "nitch") The role a creature plays in its ecosystem (e.g., squirrels eat acorns, plant oak trees, store food [and ARE food!] for other creatures, provide a home for many parasites, build nests others may use, or use nests others have built, nourish decomposers, alert other animals to danger, etc.)

nitrogen cycle — The circular flow (recycling) of nitrogen atoms through the ecosystem (from N_2 in the air through nitrogen fixers and nitrifying bacteria in the soil, into plants, and animals and people, through decomposers and back to the soil, and back to the air through de-nitrifying bacteria).

obligate — Necessary for survival, such as the dependence of a liver fluke or virus on it host. (See also *facultative*.)

omnivore — Eats both plants and meat.

overturn — In a large lake or sea, circulation of oxygen from above and nutrients from below when surface waters sink by both cooling to 39° F (4° C) in the fall and warming to that temperature in the spring.

ozone — (1) A form of oxygen including three atoms, O_3; (2) A harmful gas that, in smog near the ground, destroys lung tissue; (3) A helpful gas high in the stratosphere that absorbs ultraviolet (UV) radiation that would otherwise increase skin cancer and do other harm (see also *ozone hole*).

ozone hole — (1) Seasonal variation in the amount of stratospheric ozone, especially over Antarctica; (2) A primary factor in the belief that chemicals once in hair sprays and refrigerators (CFCs) that can rapidly break down ozone in the lab might somehow be getting into the stratosphere over Antarctica; (3) A primary factor in the fear (based on little science) that CFCs will destroy the earth's stratospheric layer of ozone, thus removing our ultraviolet radiation shield and dooming untold numbers of earthlings to death by skin cancer. (See pages 102–103.)

parasitism — ("+-") *Symbiosis* in which one species (the parasite) benefits and the other (the host) is harmed; liver flukes and some viruses and bacteria that cause human diseases may have resulted from mutations in our fallen world disrupting relationships originally created for our benefit (see pages 95–96).

pheromones — Hormones released into the environment by one organism to influence the behavior of others of its kind, including sex attractants produced by male moths and growth inhibitors secreted by plant roots.

photoperiod — Relative length of day and night, with short nights and long days in the summer and long nights and short days in the winter in the northern hemisphere.

photosynthesis — The process by which amazingly complex machinery in green plant cells is designed to use light energy to combine carbon dioxide and water to form sugar and release oxygen:
$$6CO_2 + 6H_2O \rightarrow C_6H_{12}O_6 + 6O_2.$$

phytochrome — A pigment in plants that slowly changes after sunset from active to inactive, slowly "ticking off" the length of night to help long-night (short-day) and short-night (long-day) plants "clock" the proper time for flowering, fruiting, leaf drop, etc.

pioneer — The first stage in ecological *succession*, e.g., *lichens* that can colonize bare rock, or beach grasses that begin sand dune succession.

plankton — Floating microscopic plants (phytoplankton) and animals (zooplankton) basic to aquatic food chains.

pollutant — Anything that disrupts proper ecological balance.

pollution solution — Since almost all ecological problems can be solved scientifically, the real problem is greed and selfishness, a lack of concern for others, and for the home our Father gave us — so the real "pollution solution" is Jesus Christ, living and loving others and our home, and following His example in the power of His Spirit.

population explosion — (1) The rapid and continuing increase in the human population that began in the early 1900s with major medical advances; (2) fear that unrestricted birth of babies will destroy the planet (even though all six-billion-plus people living today could fit in one county without touching one another; (3) failure to follow God's command to scatter out, resulting in a few areas with horribly heavy populations and vast open areas that would make pleasant homes for many, many more people.

pre-Flood ecology — Science and/or Scripture suggest that the world before Noah's flood may have differed from ours in several ways: (1) Milder climate pole-to-pole due to the *greenhouse effect* of greater CO_2 levels and perhaps a water vapor canopy; (2) springs bringing mineral-rich water up to plant roots instead of rainwater *leaching* minerals away; (3) greater plant and animal diversity, larger sizes, and longer life spans; (4) far fewer mutational diseases and defects; (5) much ecological variety, but absence of vast ice sheets, deserts, and high mountain rain shadows, etc.; (6) perhaps less difference between salt water and fresh; (7) perhaps one continent and many shallow inland seas, etc. (See pages 81–82.)

predator-prey feedback — Means of population regulation in our corrupted creation in which *predators* reduce prey populations until fewer prey reduce the predator population and then increase in numbers to start the cycle over again; a result of struggle and death after mankind's *sin*, NOT a created means of population balance like territoriality. (See pages 60–62.)

predators — *Carnivores*, like lions, that hunt live animals (prey) and kill and eat them; absent before mankind's sin and after Christ's return, but they help to regulate prey populations in our fallen world.

producers — Food makers; the green plants designed to use sunlight energy, CO_2, and H_2O to make food (sugar) and O_2 for themselves and all other life forms through photosynthesis; the base of all food chains.

rain shadow — The dry regions produced downwind (leeward) of mountains because cooling air loses its moisture on the upwind (windward) side.

renewable — A resource that can be replaced, such as trees that can be planted to take the place of those used to make paper (in contrast to resources that cannot be replaced as fast as they are used, such as oil and iron ore).

Rhizobium — A nitrogen-fixing bacterium that lives (in mutualistic symbiosis) in root nodules of *legumes*, enriching the soil as these plants grow; farmers may add spores of these bacteria to legume seeds they plant to increase soil fertility.

red tide — Explosive growth (*bloom*) of reddish-brown microscopic organisms (dinoflagellates) that produce a nerve poison that kills fish.

Redeemer — See *Christ*.

reef — Fantastic limestone (calcium carbonate) "castles" formed when certain kinds of corals, clams, algae, sponges, etc., cement themselves together in warm, shallow seas; may be fringing (along shore), barrier (offshore, parallel to coast), or an atoll (circular, around submerged peak); provide homes to many beautiful, colorful fish and sea creatures.

respiration (cellular respiration) — The fantastic process with many steps by which the living cells of plants, animals, most microbes, and people are designed to burn sugar with oxygen to produce energy and release carbon dioxide and water (which green plants "recycle" in photosynthesis):
$$C_6H_{12}O_6 + 6O_2 \rightarrow 6CO_2 + 6H_2O + \text{energy}$$

ritualistic combat — Instinctive ways living things defend their territories without fighting to the death, such as "singing duels" among birds.

SAD (seasonal affective disorder) — Feelings of sluggishness and/or depression during seasons of long nights or heavy cloudiness experienced by people who need a lot of sunlight to suppress the production of sleep-inducing melanin from the pineal gland; can be treated with special lights that mimic the sun's wavelengths.

sand dune succession — Ecological progression from beach sand to beech-maple forest as sand is anchored, soil enriched with *humus*, and shade and moisture are increased (sand to beach to grass to sun-tolerant trees to shade-tolerant trees to pines to oak-hickory to beech-maple).

scavengers — Animals, like buzzards or vultures, that eat other animals only after they have died.

seasons — Yearly cycle of variation in day length and temperature, with greatest differences near the poles; established by God on creation day 4, apparently by His giving the earth's axis a tilt. The seasons are opposite north and south of the equator, e.g., Australia is in summer while Canada is in winter.

second law of thermodynamics — (1) The scientific observation that all net changes in nature always occur with a loss of useful energy, order, or information; (2) the scientific description of a corrupted creation in a "bondage to decay" between mankind's *sin* and *Christ's* return; (3) the scientific principle that means any increase in order or information requires both an energy-harnessing system (e.g., photosynthesis or a living egg cell) and an outside energy source (e.g., the sun) which is losing more energy than the growing system is gaining (e.g., the sun is losing four and a half million tons per second to power life on earth).

secondary succession — Ecological re-growth starting with a richer biological base (e.g., an abandoned field or lawn; an area damaged by fire, wind, or water; or the world after Noah's flood) so that it occurs faster than primary succession on a barren, mineral environment.

seral stages — The communities between the *pioneer* and *climax* stages in ecological succession, such as the "fern stage" between *lichens* and forest in *bare rock succession*.

sigmoid (s-shaped) growth curve — An s-shaped graph showing the tendency for population growth to start slowly (lag phase), then increase rapidly (log phase), before reaching a maximum (level phase).

sin — (1) Our selfish failure in thought, word, or deed to accept our Creator's commands as acts of His love designed to help us be our best; (2) mankind's rebellion against God and rejection of His Word that brought defects, disease, death, and disaster into the world that God had created "all very good." (See *corruption*.)

soil — One of several kinds of substances composed of varying amounts of minerals (with fragments), decaying plants (humus), living things (e.g., microbes and worms), moisture, and air space (i.e., more than just "dirt").

"Spaceship Earth" — A name that reminds us that God created our planet with all the matter and energy we need for long-term space travel around our sun.

steno- — Prefix used for creatures that can only survive within a narrow range of some environmental factor (e.g., stenohaline and stenothermal species would die if the amount of salt [-haline] or temperature [-thermal] in the environment changed much).

stewardship — The Christian principle that those God puts in charge are to serve and bring out the best in those under their care, which includes God's command to "*till and keep*" or, after *sin*, to "*heal and restore*" the earth as a "garden of delight"; if Christians followed *Christ's* example of "servant leadership" (stewardship), the earth would be better, rather than worse, for mankind's presence.

succession — (1) An orderly series of ecological changes that happens when organisms in one ecosystem change their environment in ways that pave the way for the next ecosystem in progression from *pioneer* through *seral* stages to the final *climax* community; (2) An observable, simple-to-complex development of life in an area over tens or hundreds of years based on migration and changing environments, unlike *evolution*, which is an imagined simple-to-complex development of life over millions of years based on *mutation* and one kind of life changing into others.

sustainer — God's role as the One who daily, faithfully takes care of His creation through the continuing, regular operation of the universe (on which science depends), in contrast to God's role as *Creator* seen in the completed, supernatural acts by which the universe originated.

symbiosis — Two species living in particularly close dependence on each other (e.g., cleaning symbiosis, in which predator fish get their mouths cleaned by cleaner fish, who get a free meal of food fragments in return. (See *mutualism*, *commensalism*, and *parasitism*, the three kinds of symbiosis.)

symbolic territory — A small breeding/nesting site in a restricted area that represents (symbolizes) a much larger feeding area, (e.g., walruses restricting breeding to small parts of only certain beaches means there will be plenty of food for all as they cruise through the ocean.)

taiga (coniferous forest) — *Biome* of plants (spruce and fir) and animals (moose) designed for the cold environment circling the globe through North America and Eurasia.

ten percent rule — On average, only about 10 percent of the food available at one level in a food chain is transferred to the next (so that, for example, 100 tons of grass might support 10 tons of cattle, and only 1 ton of wolves).

territorial marking — The way creatures warn others of their kind that a certain area has been claimed, including singing by birds, urinating by dogs, and secreting growth inhibitors by the roots of some desert plants.

territoriality — A created way of maintaining population balance using complex God-given *instincts* for marking territory and for defending it by *ritualistic combat* so that, without any death, creatures can "multiply and fill" an area without over-filling it. (See pages 63–66.)

thermocline — Boundary between upper warm water and lower cold water, formed because water is "heaviest" (densest) at 39° F (4° C) and sinks.

thermophile "heat living" — Plant, animal, or microbe designed to thrive at high temperatures like those in hot springs.

tide pools — Pockets in rocky shorelines that hold water even at low tide, providing excellent places to study fascinating creatures.

"till and keep" — God's stewardship command (Genesis 2:15), telling our first parents to keep and develop the home their Heavenly Father gave them as a "garden of delight."

top carnivore — A meat-eating animal not usually eaten by any other creature while it's alive.

tropical rain forest — *Biome* with tall trees and vines forming a dense canopy over a dark forest floor with very poor soils due to abundant rain washing away minerals.

tropisms — Directed growth movements in plants usually controlled by hormones called *auxins*, e.g., growth of stems toward light (positive phototropism) or up away from the earth (negative geotropism).

tundra — Treeless, icy *biome* with shallow, marshy soil above the permafrost that serves as home for many mosquitoes and migratory birds during the long days of arctic summer.

vernalization — A period of cold treatment used to remove inhibitors to sprouting or budding in plants, and pupa (cocoon) development in insects.

"war of nature" — What Charles Darwin called the time, chance, struggle, and death that evolutionists accept as a substitute for the Bible's record of *creation*, *corruption*, *catastrophe*, and *Christ*.

web of life — A name that reminds us that God created all living things and their environment to work together so that touching one "strand" affects all the others in the "web."

ZPG (zero population growth) — The point at which birth and death rates balance, which, at 2.1 children per couple, has already been reached in "developed" countries such as the United States of America.

More from the Exploring Series

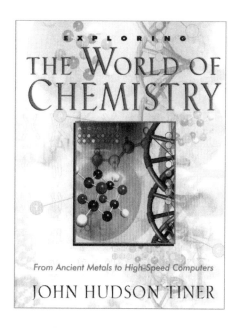

Exploring the World of Chemistry

Chemistry is an amazing branch of science that affects us every day. Without chemistry, there would be no rubber tires, no tin cans, no televisions, no microwave ovens, no wax paper. Find out why pure gold is not used for jewelry or coins. Join Humphry Davy as he made many chemical discoveries, and learn how they shortened his life. See how people in the 1870s could jump over the top of the Washington Monument. Includes many illustrations, biographical information, chapter tests, and an index.

ISBN: 0-89051-295-7
144 pages
$13.99
8-1/2 x 11

Available at Christian bookstores nationwide

More from the Exploring Series

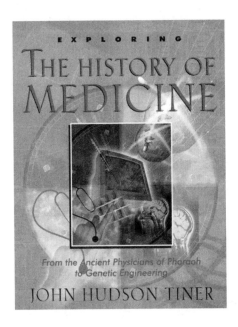

Exploring the History of Medicine

From surgery to vaccines, man has made great strides in the field of medicine. Quality of life has improved dramatically in the last few decades alone, but we should not forget that God provided humans with minds and resources to bring about these advances. A biblical perspective of healing and the use of medicine provides the best foundation for treating diseases and injury. The fascinating history of medicine comes alive in this book, providing students with a healthy dose of facts, mini-biographies, and vintage illustrations. Includes chapter tests and index.

ISBN: 0-89051-248-5
168 pages
$13.99
8-1/2 x 11

Available at Christian bookstores nationwide

More from the
Exploring Series

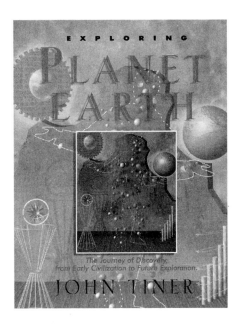

Exploring Planet Earth

Blending a creationism perspective of history with definitions of terms and identification of famous explorers, scientists, etc., this book gives an excellent initial knowledge of people and places, encouraging the reader to continue their studies in-depth. Supplemented with photographs, illustrations, chapter review activities, and an index.

ISBN: 0-89051-178-0
168 pages
$13.99
8-1/2 x 11

Available at Christian bookstores nationwide